Gay Love Poetry

NEIL POWELL is the author of four books of poetry, a novel, a study of contemporary English poetry and a critical biography, *Roy Fuller: Writer and Society* (1995). He lives in Suffolk.

Gay Love Poetry

Edited by Neil Powell

ROBINSON
London

Robinson Publishing Ltd
7 Kensington Church Court
London W8 4SP

First published by Robinson Publishing Ltd 1997

A copy of the British Library Cataloguing in Publication Data is
available from the British Library.

ISBN 1–85487–917–0

Printed and bound in the EC

10 9 8 7 6 5 4 3 2 1

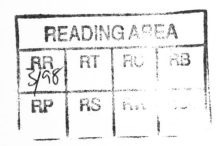

for Nick: vanishing trick

CONTENTS

III LADS' LOVE

V BORDERLINES

VI   IN MEMORIAM

INTRODUCTION

An anthologist should declare his principles, if only to assist his critics in their task of demonstrating how thoroughly he has betrayed them. The first thing to say about *Gay Love Poetry* is that I've taken liberties – pardonable ones, I hope – with my title: 'gay' has had the sense of 'male homosexual' for a good deal longer than its enemies pretend, certainly since the late nineteenth century, but for the purpose of this book I have applied its convenient shorthand to poetry written as far back as the eighth century BC; and I have allowed 'love' to encompass as wide a range of affectionate relationships as possible. That double inclusiveness has enabled me to gather together a more various and more interesting group of poems than is usual in anthologies of this sort.

The poems are arranged in six broadly thematic sections, each with an introductory note; within each section they are printed in chronological order of their authors' births, although I've made a few deliberate exceptions among twentieth-century poets. While the thematic groupings offer intriguing juxtapositions, the sequences within them provide some sense of historical development. The first and last sections, 'Nature Boys' and 'In Memoriam', essentially comprise pastorals and elegies – the two oldest and most enduring forms of gay love poetry – while three others explore somewhat looser categories; the sixth, 'Borderlines', consists mainly of poems which may not have been conceived by their authors as about gay love but which have certainly been so interpreted by grateful readers.

For reasons to do equally with the histories of homosexuality and of literature, three eras are predominant here: the classical age in Greece and Rome; the sixteenth and early seventeenth centuries in England; and the period from the mid-nineteenth century to the present. In the first two cases, I have included both the work of major writers and some lesser-known and possibly unexpected pieces; in pre-eighteenth-century texts, spellings which might be obstructive to the general reader have been modernized. The third is deliberately weighted towards poems published or collected here for the first time, rather than those which are readily accessible elsewhere; it is also drawn more from Britain than from America, partly because these are the writers I know best, but also because several anthologies of gay poetry have appeared in the USA during recent years and my guess is that readers there will welcome the less familiar work included here.

One of the pleasures (at first hoped-for rather than confidently anticipated) of assembling this book has been discovering the quality and diversity of recent writing which would be offered for it: among the newly collected poems here are several which seem to me outstanding as well as others, perhaps less completely distinguished, which I've liked for particular qualities – for catching their specific moment or for an irresistible line or image. In other words, every poem has earned its place. Inevitably, there are a few missing persons – writers who didn't receive or reply to my letters, who weren't happy about contributing, or whose publishers were unwilling to grant affordable permissions – but I'd like to suspect that on the whole they may regret having missed this particular party. I am especially sorry that W.H. Auden's American publishers (Random House, Inc.) refused to allow his work to appear in this book.

I am grateful to all the poets, translators and publishers who have allowed material to appear in this anthology; to Mark Crean at Robinson Publishing for commissioning the book; and to Steve Anthony, Peter Daniels, Thom Gunn, Francis King, David Kinloch, Joel Lane, Michael Schmidt, Ivor C. Treby, Gregory Woods and Martin Wright for useful suggestions and advice.

N.P.

I NATURE BOYS

The pastoral provides one of the oldest strands of gay love poetry. The classical tradition of rustic love which is often unreciprocated or obstructed or at least delayed is represented here by Theocritus and Virgil. It was rediscovered and adapted by major writers of the English renaissance such as Sidney, Marlowe and Shakespeare; as well as work by these three, I have included in full Richard Barnfield's splendid long poem 'The Affectionate Shepherd'.

The Greek myth of Ganymede also surfaces and resurfaces here, either glancingly or centrally, in Marlowe's *Hero and Leander* and the opening of *Dido Queen of Carthage* (grouped here for that reason, though it isn't otherwise a pastoral scene), Shakespeare's *As You Like It* and Roger Finch's 'The Rape of Ganymede'. The *As You Like It* extract, incidentally, may at first seem an odd choice: but it is a deliciously concise example of the gender-masking which so permeates Shakespeare's comedies as well as a moment of high pastoral pastiche.

Wilde's 'Charmides', though not wholly a gay text, was the author's own 'favourite poem ... my best ... the most perfect and finished'; the very beguiling extract printed here perhaps suggests why.

THEOCRITUS

Translated by Thomas Creech

Idyll 23

An amorous shepherd lov'd a charming boy,
As fair as thought could frame, or wish enjoy;
Unlike his soul, ill-natur'd and unkind,
An angel's body with a fury's mind:
How great a God Love was, he scorn'd to know,
How sharp his arrows, and how strong his bow,
What raging wounds he scatters here below.
In his address and talk fierce, rude, untame,
He gave no comfort to the shepherd's flame:
No cherry lips, no rose his cheeks did dye,
No pleasing fire did sparkle in his eye,
Where eager thoughts with fainting virtue strove,
No soft discourse, nor kiss to ease his love:
But as a lion on the Lybian plain
Looks on his hunters, he beheld the swain:
His lips still pouting, and his eyes unkind,
His forehead too was rough as was his mind;
His colour gone, and every pleasing grace
Beset by fury had forsook his face;
Yet midst his passion, midst his frowns he mov'd,
As these were charms he was the more belov'd:
But when o'ercome he could endure no more,
He came and wept before the hated door,
He wept and pin'd, he hung his sickly head,
The threshold kiss'd, and thus at last he said:
'Ah cruel fair, and of a Tigress born!
Ah stony boy, compos'd of frowns and scorn:
Unworthy of my love, this rope receive,
The last and welcom'st present I can give:

I'll never vex thee more, I'll cease to woe,
And whether you condemn'd, I'll freely go,
Where certain cures for love, as stories tell,
Where dismal shades, and dark oblivion dwell:
Yet did I drink the whole forgetful stream,
It would not drown my love, nor quench my flame:
Thy cruel doors I bid my last adieu,
Know what will come, and you shall find it true:
The day is fair but quickly yields to shades,
The lily white, but when 'tis pluck'd it fades:
The violet lovely, but it withers soon,
Youth's beauty charming, but 'tis quickly gone:
The time shall come when you, proud boy, shall prove
The heat of passion, and the rage of love:
Then shall thy soul melt through thy weeping eye,
Whilst all shall smile, and you unpitied die.
Yet grant one kindness, and I ask no more,
When you shall see me hanging at the door
Do not go proudly by, forbear to smile,
But stay, sweet boy, and gaze, and weep a while;
Then take me down, and whilst some tears are shed,
Thy own soft garment o'er my body spread,
And grant one kiss, one kiss when I am dead:
Ne'er fear, for you may safely grant me this,
I shan't revive though you could love and kiss:
Then dig a grave, there let my love be laid,
And when you part, say thrice, "My friend is dead",
Or else go further on to please my ghost,
And cry, "My best, my dearest friend is lost":
And on my monument inscribe this rhyme,
The witness of my love and of thy crime,
This shepherd died for love, stay Stranger here,
And weep, and cry, He lov'd a cruel fair.'
This said, he roll'd a stone, a mighty stone,
Fate lent a hand behind, and push'd it on:
High by the wall, on this he panting rose,

And tied, and fitted well the fatal noose:
Then from the place on which before he stood
He slipp'd, and hung the door's unhappy load:
The boy came forth, and with a scornful mien
And smiling look beheld the tragic scene;
'Hang there,' said he, 'but O how I despise
So base, so mean a trophy of my eyes!
The proudest kings should fall by my disdain,
Too noble to be lost upon a swain.'
This said, he turn'd, and as he turn'd his head
His garments were polluted by the dead,
Thence to the plays and to the baths did move,
The bath was sacred to the God of Love;
For there he stood in comely majesty,
Smiles on his cheeks, and softness in his eye,
That part of th'marble wrought into his breast
By power divine was softer than the rest,
To show how pity did exactly suit
With love, and was his darling attribute:
The God leap forth, and dash'd the boy, the wound
Let out his soul, and as it fled he groan'd.
    'Hail Lovers, hail, see here the scornful dies,
A just, and acceptable sacrifice,
Be kind, and Love for mutual Love return,
For see the God takes vengeance on my scorn.'

VIRGIL
Translated by John Dryden

Pastoral II

Young Corydon, the unhappy shepherd swain,
The fair Alexis loved, but loved in vain;
And undernearth the beechen shade, alone,
Thus to the woods and mountains made his moan:
Is this, unkind Alexis, my reward?
And must I die unpitied, and unheard?
Now the green lizard in the grove is laid;
The sheep enjoy the coolness of the shade:
And Thestylis wild thyme and garlic beats,
For harvest hinds, o'erspent with toil and heats;
While in the scorching sun I trace in vain
The flying footsteps o'er the burning plain.
The creaking locusts with my voice conspire,
They fried with heat, and I with fierce desire.
How much more easy was it to sustain
Proud Amaryllis, and her haughty reign;
The scorns of young Menalcas, once my care,
Though he was black, and thou art heavenly fair!
Trust not too much to that enchanting face:
Beauty's a charm; but soon the charm will pass.
White lilies lie neglected on the plain,
While dusky hyacinths for use remain.
My passion is thy scorn; nor wilt thou know
What wealth I have, what gifts I can bestow;
What stores my dairies and my folds contain –
A thousand lambs that wander on the plain,
New milk that, all the winter, never fails,
And, all the summer, overflows the pails.
Amphion sung not sweeter to his herd,

When summoned stones the Theban turrets reared.
Nor am I so deformed; for late I stood
Upon the margin of the briny flood:
The winds were still; and, if the glass be true,
With Daphnis I may vie, though judged by you.
O leave the noisy town: O come and see
Our country cots, and live content with me!
To wound the flying deer, and from their cotes
With me to drive a-field the browsing goats;
To pipe and sing, and, in our country strain,
To copy, or perhaps contend with Pan.
Pan taught to join with wax unequal reeds;
Pan loves the shepherds, and their flocks he feeds.
Nor scorn the pipe: Amyntas, to be taught,
With all his kisses would my skill have bought.
Of seven smooth joints a mellow pipe I have,
Which with his dying breath Damoetas gave,
And said, 'This, Corydon, I leave to thee;
For only thou deserv'st it after me.'
His eyes Amyntas durst not upward lift;
For much he grudged the praise, but more the gift.
Besides, two kids, that in the valley strayed,
I found by chance, and to my fold conveyed;
They drain two bagging udders every day;
And these shall be companions of thy play;
Both, flecked with white, the true Arcadian strain,
Which Thestylis had often begged in vain:
And she shall have them, if again she sues,
Since you the giver and the gift refuse.
Come to my longing arms, my lovely care!
And take the presents which the nymphs prepare.
White lilies in full canisters they bring,
With all the glories of the purple spring.
The daughters of the flood have searched the mead
For violets pale, and cropped the poppy's head,
The short narcissus and fair daffodil,

Pansies to please the sight, and cassia sweet to smell:
And set soft hyacinths with iron-blue,
To shade marsh marigolds of shining hue;
Some bound in order, others loosely strewed,
To dress thy bower, and trim thy new abode.
Myself will search our planted grounds at home,
For downy peaches and the glossy plum;
And thrash the chestnuts in the neighbouring grove,
Such as my Amaryllis used to love.
The laurel and the myrtle sweets agree;
And both in nosegays shall be bound for thee.
Ah, Corydon! ah, poor unhappy swain!
Alexis will thy homely gifts disdain;
Nor, shouldst thou offer all thy little store,
Will rich Iolas yield, but offer more.
What have I done, to name that wealthy swain!
So powerful are his presents, mine so mean!
The board amidst my crystal streams I bring:
And southern winds to blast my flowery spring.
Ah, cruel creature! whom dost thou despise?
The gods, to live in woods, have left the skies:
And godlike Paris, in the Idaean grove,
To Priam's wealth preferred Oenone's love.
In cities, which she built, let Pallas reign;
Towers are for gods, but forests for the swain.
The greedy lioness the wolf pursues,
The wolf the kid, the wanton kid the browse;
Alexis, thou art chased by Corydon:
All follow several games, and each his own.
See, from afar the fields no longer smoke;
The sweating steers, unharnessed from the yoke,
Bring, as in triumph, back the crooked plough;
The shadows lengthen as the sun goes low;
Cool breezes now the raging heats remove;
Ah! cruel heaven, that made no cure for love!
I wish for balmy sleep, but wish in vain:

Love has no bounds in pleasure, or in pain.
What frenzy, shepherd, has thy soul possessed?
The vineyard lies half-pruned, and half-undressed
Quench, Corydon, thy long-unanswered fire,
Mind what the common wants of life require:
On willow twigs employ thy weaving care;
And find an easier love, though not so fair.

VIRGIL

Translated by John Dryden

from Pastoral VIII

Now take your turns, ye muses, to rehearse
His friend's complaints, and mighty magic verse.
   'Bring running water: bind those altars round
With fillets, and with vervain strew the ground:
Make fat with frankincense the sacred fires,
To reinflame my Daphnis with desires.
'Tis done; we want but verse. Restore, my charms,
My lingering Daphnis to my longing arms.
   Pale Phoebe, drawn by verse, from heaven descends;
And Circe changed with charms Ulysses' friends.
Verse breaks the ground, and penetrates the brake,
And in the winding cavern splits the snake.
Verse fires the frozen veins. Restore, my charms,
My lingering Daphnis to my longing arms.
   Around his waxen image first I wind
Three woollen fillets, of three colours joined;
Thrice bind about his thrice-devoted head,
Which round the sacred altar thrice is led.
Unequal numbers please the gods. My charms,
Restore my Daphnis to my longing arms.
   Knit with three knots the fillets: knit them strait;
Then say, 'These knots to Love I consecrate!'
Haste, Amaryllis, haste! Restore, my charms,
My lovely Daphnis to my longing arms.
   As fire this figure hardens, made of clay,
And this of wax with fire consumes away;
Such let the soul of cruel Daphnis be –
Hard to the rest of women, soft to me.
Crumble the sacred mole of salt and corn:

Next in the fire the bays with brimstone burn
And, while it crackles in the sulphur, say,
'This I for Daphnis burnt; thus Daphnis burnt away!
This laurel is his fate.' Restore, my charms
My lovely Daphnis to my longing arms.

As when the raging heifer, through the grove,
Stung with desire, pursues her wandering love;
Faint at the last, she seeks the weedy pools,
To quench her thirst, and on the rushes rolls,
Careless of night, unmindful to return;
Such fruitless fires perfidious Daphnis burn,
While I so scorn his love! Restore, my charms,
My lingering Daphnis to my longing arms.

These garments once were his, and left to me,
The pledges of his promised loyalty,
Which underneath my threshold I bestow.
These pawns, O sacred earth! to me my Daphnis owe,
As these were his, so mine is he. My charms,
Restore their lingering lord to my deluded arms.

These poisonous plants, for magic use designed
(The noblest and the best of all the baneful kind),
Old Moeris brought me from the Pontic strand,
And culled the mischief of a bounteous land.
Smeared with those powerful juices, on the plain
He howls a wolf among the hungry train;
And oft the might necromancer boasts,
With these to call from tombs the stalking ghosts,
And from the roots to tear the standing corn,
Which, whirled aloft, to distant fields is borne:
Such is the strength of spells. Restore, my charms,
My lingering Daphnis to my longing arms.

Bear out these ashes; cast them in the brook;
Cast backwards o'er your head; nor turn your look:
Since neither gods nor godlike verse can move,
Break out, ye smothered fires, and kindle smothered love.
Exert your utmost power, my lingering charms;

And force my Daphnis to my longing arms.
    See, while my last endeavours I delay,
The waking ashes rise, and round our altars play!
Run to the threshold, Amaryllis – hark!
Our Hylax opens, and begins to bark.
Good heaven! may lovers what they wish believe?
Or dream their wishes, and those dreams deceive?
No more! my Daphnis comes! no more, my charms!
He comes, he runs, he leaps to my desiring arms.'

[87–159]

SIR PHILIP SIDNEY

'My true love hath my heart, and I have his ... '

My true love hath my heart, and I have his,
By just exchange one for the other given.
I hold his dear, and mine he cannot miss:
There never was a better bargain driven.
His heart in me keeps me and him in one;
My heart in him his thoughts and senses guides;
He loves my heart, for once it was his own;
I cherish his, because in me it bides.
His heart his wound received from my sight;
My heart was wounded with his wounded heart;
For as from me on him his hurt did light,
So still, methought, in me his hurt did smart;
    Both equal hurt, in this change sought our bliss:
    My true love hath my heart, and I have his.

CHRISTOPHER MARLOWE

from Hero and Leander

O none but gods have power their love to hide,
Affection by the count'nance is descried.
The light of hidden fire itself discovers,
And love that is concealed betrays poor lovers.
His secret flame apparently was seen,
Leander's father knew where he had been,
And for the same mildly rebuked his son,
Thinking to quench the sparkles new begun.
But love resisted once grows passionate,
And nothing more than counsel lovers hate.
For as a hot proud horse highly disdains
To have his head controlled, but breaks the reins,
Spits forth the ringled bit, and with his hooves
Checks the submissive ground: so he that loves,
The more he is restrained, the worse he fares.
What is it now, but mad Leander dares?
'O Hero, Hero!' thus he cried full oft,
And then he got him to a rock aloft,
Where having spied her tower, long stared he on't,
And prayed the narrow toiling Hellespont
To part in twain, that he might come and go,
But still the rising billows answered 'No.'
With that he stripped him to the ivory skin,
And crying, 'Love, I come,' leapt lively in.
Whereat the sapphire-visaged god grew proud,
And made his capering Triton sound aloud,
Imagining that Ganymede, displeased,
Had left the heavens; therefore on him he seized.
Leander strived, the waves about him wound,
And pulled him to the bottom, where the ground

Was strewed with pearl, and in low coral groves
Sweet singing mermaids sported with their loves
On heaps of heavy gold, and took great pleasure
To spurn in careless sort the shipwrack treasure.
For here the stately azure palace stood
Where kingly Neptune and his train abode.
The lusty god embraced him, called him love,
And swore he never should return to Jove.
But when he knew it was not Ganymede,
For under water he was almost dead,
He heaved him up, and looking on his face,
Beat down the bold waves with his triple mace,
Which mounted up, intending to have kissed him,
And fell in drops like tears because they missed him.
Leander, being up, began to swim,
And, looking back, saw Neptune follow him;
Whereat aghast, the poor soul 'gan to cry,
'O let me visit Hero ere I die!'
The god put Helle's bracelet on his arm,
And swore the sea should never do him harm.
He clapped his plump cheeks, with his tresses played,
And smiling wantonly, his love betrayed.
He watched his arms, and as they opened wide
At every stroke, betwixt them would he slide
And steal a kiss, and then run out and dance,
And as he turned, cast many a lustful glance,
And threw him gaudy toys to please his eye,
And dive into the water, and there pry
Upon his breast, his thighs, and every limb,
And up again, and close beside him swim,
And talk of love. Leander made reply,
'You are deceived, I am no woman, I.'
Thereat smiled Neptune, and then told a tale,
How that a shepherd, sitting in a vale,
Played with a boy so lovely fair and kind,
As for his love both earth and heaven pined;

That of the cooling river durst not drink,
Lest water-nymphs should pull him from the brink;
And when he sported in the fragrant lawns,
Goat-footed satyrs and up-staring fauns
Would steal him thence. Ere half this tale was done,
'Aye me,' Leander cried, 'th'enamoured sun,
That now should shine on Thetis' glassy bower,
Descends upon my radiant Hero's tower.
O! that these tardy arms of mine were wings!'
And as he spake, upon the waves he springs.
Neptune was angry that he gave no ear,
And in his heart revenging malice bare:
He flung at him his mace, but as it went,
He called it in, for love made him repent.
The mace returning back, his own hand hit,
As meaning to be venged for darting it.
When this fresh bleeding wound Leander viewed,
His colour went and came, as if he rued
The grief which Neptune felt. In gentle breasts
Relenting thoughts, remorse and pity rests.
And who have hard hearts and obdurate minds,
But vicious, harebrained, and illit'rate hinds?
The god, seeing him with pity to be movèd,
Thereon concluded that he was belovèd.
(Love is too full of faith, too credulous,
With folly and false hope deluding us.)
Wherefore Leander's fancy to surprise,
To the rich Ocean for gifts he flies.
'Tis wisdom to give much, a gift prevails
When deep persuading oratory fails.

   [II. 131–226]

CHRISTOPHER MARLOWE

from Dido Queen of Carthage

Here the curtains draw. There is discovered Jupiter dandling
Ganymede upon his knee, and Mercury lying asleep.

Jupiter	Come, gentle Ganymede, and play with me.
	I love thee well, say Juno what she will.
Ganymede	I am much better for your worthless love,
	That will not shield me from her shrewish blows.
	Today, whenas I filled into your cups
	And held the cloth of pleasance whiles you drank,
	She reached me such a rap for that I spilled,
	As made the blood run down about mine ears.
Jupiter	What! Dares she strike the darling of my thoughts?
	By Saturn's soul and this earth-threat'ning hair,
	That, shaken thrice, makes nature's buildings
	quake,
	I vow, if she but once frown on thee more,
	To hang her, meteor-like, 'twixt heaven and earth
	And bind her hand and foot with golden cords,
	As once I did for harming Hercules.
Ganymede	Might I but see that pretty sport afoot,
	O, how would I with Helen's brother laugh
	And bring the gods to wonder at the game.
	Sweet Jupiter, if e'er I pleased thine eye
	Or seemèd fair, walled in with eagle's wings,
	Grace my immortal beauty with this boon,
	And I will spend my time in thy bright arms.
Jupiter	What is't, sweet wag, I should deny thy youth,
	Whose face reflects such pleasure to mine eyes,
	As I, exhaled with thy fire-darting beams,
	Have oft driven back the horses of the night,

Whenas they would have haled thee from my sight.
Sit on my knee and call for thy content;
Control proud fate and cut the thread of time.
Why, are not all the gods at thy command
And heaven and earth the bounds of thy delight?
Vulcan shall dance to make thee laughing sport,
And my nine daughters sing when thou art sad.
From Juno's bird I'll pluck her spotted pride
To make thee fans wherewith to cool thy face,
And Venus' swans shall shed their silver down
To sweeten out the slumbers of thy bed.
Hermes no more shall show the world his wings,
If that thy fancy in his feathers dwell,
But, as this one, I'll tear them all from him,
                    [He plucks a feather from Mercury's wings.]
Do thou but say, 'Their colour pleaseth me.'
Hold here, my little love. These linkèd gems
                              [He gives jewels.]
My Juno ware upon her marriage day,
Put thou about thy neck, my own sweetheart,
And trick thy arms and shoulders with my theft.

Ganymede   I would have a jewel for mine ear
And a fine brooch to put in my hat,
And then I'll hug with you an hundred times.

Jupiter   And shall have, Ganymede, if thou wilt be my
                love.

[II:I:I–49]

CHRISTOPHER MARLOWE

The Passionate Shepherd to his Love

Come live with me, and be my love,
And we will all the pleasures prove
That valleys, groves, hills and fields,
Woods, or steepy mountain yields.

And we will sit upon the rocks,
Seeing the shepherds feed their flocks
By shallow rivers, to whose falls
Melodious birds sing madrigals.

And I will make thee beds of roses,
And a thousand fragrant posies,
A cap of flowers, and a kirtle
Embroidered all with leaves of myrtle.

A gown made of the finest wool
Which from our pretty lambs we pull,
Fair linèd slippers for the cold
With buckles of the purest gold.

A belt of straw and ivy-buds,
With coral clasps and amber studs,
And if these pleasures may thee move,
Come live with me, and be my love.

The shepherd swains shall dance and sing
For thy delight each May morning.
If these delights thy mind may move,
Then live with me, and be my love.

WILLIAM SHAKESPEARE

Sonnet 99

The forward violet thus did I chide:
Sweet thief, whence didst thou steal thy sweet that smells
If not from my love's breath? The purple pride
Which on thy soft cheek for complexion dwells
In my love's veins thou hast too grossly dyed.
The lily I condemnèd for thy hand,
And buds of marjoram had stol'n thy hair,
The roses fearfully on thorns did stand,
One blushing shame, another white despair;
A third, nor red nor white, had stol'n of both,
And to his robb'ry had annexed thy breath;
But for his theft, in pride of all his growth
A vengeful canker eat him up to death.
    More flowers I noted, yet I none could see,
    But sweet or colour it had stol'n from thee.

WILLIAM SHAKESPEARE

from As You Like It

Phebe	Good shepherd, tell this youth what 'tis to love.
Silvius	It is to be all made of sighs and tears,
	And so am I for Phebe.
Phebe	And I for Ganymede.
Orlando	And I for Rosalind.
Rosalind	And I for no woman.
Silvius	It is to be all made of faith and service,
	And so am I for Phebe.
Phebe	And I for Ganymede.
Orlando	And I for Rosalind.
Rosalind	And I for no woman.
Silvius	It is to be all made of fantasy,
	All made of passion and all made of wishes,
	All adoration, duty and observance,
	All humbleness, all patience and impatience,
	All purity, all trial, all observance;
	And so am I for Phebe.
Phebe	And so am I for Ganymede.
Orlando	And so am I for Rosalind.
Rosalind	And so am I for no woman.
Phebe [to Rosalind]	
	If this be so, why blame you me to love you?
Silvius [to Phebe]	
	If this be so, why blame you me to love you?
Orlando	If this be so, why blame you me to love you?
Rosalind	Who do you speak to 'Why blame you me to
	love you?'?
Orlando	To her that is not here, nor doth not hear.
Rosalind	Pray you no more of this, 'tis like the howling
	of Irish wolves against the moon.

[V:II:82–III]

RICHARD BARNFIELD

The Affectionate Shepherd

Scarce had the morning star hid from the light
   Heaven's crimson canopy with stars bespangled,
But I began to rue th'unhappy sight
   Of that fair boy that had my heart entangled;
     Cursing the time, the place, the sense, the sin;
     I came, I saw, I viewed, I slipped in.

If it be sin to love a sweet-faced boy
   (Whose amber locks trussed up in golden trammels
Dangle adown his lovely cheeks with joy,
   When pearl and flowers his fair hair enamels)
     If it be sin to love a lovely lad,
     On then sin I, for whom my soul is sad.

His ivory-white and alabaster skin
   Is stained throughout with rare vermillion red,
Whose twinkling starry lights do never blin
   To shine on lovely Venus, beauty's bed;
     But as the lily and the blushing rose,
     So white and red on him in order grows.

Upon a time the nymphs bestirred themselves
   To try who could his beauty soonest win;
But he accounted them but all as elves,
   Except it were the fair Queen Gwendolen:
     Her he embraced, of her was he beloved,
     With plaints he proved, and with tears he moved.

But her an old man had been suitor to,
  That in his age began to dote again.
Her would he often pray, and often woo,
  When through old age enfeebled was his brain.
    But she before had loved a lusty youth
    That now was dead, the cause of all her ruth.

And thus it happened. Death and Cupid met
  Upon a time at swilling Bacchus' house,
Where dainty cates upon the board were set
  And goblets full of wine to drink carouse:
    Where Love and Death did love the liquor so
    That out they fall and to the fray they go.

And having both their quivers at their back
  Filled full of arrows; th'one of fatal steel,
The other all of gold; Death's shaft was black,
  But Love's was yellow: Fortune turned her wheel;
    And from Death's quiver fell a fatal shaft,
    That under Cupid by the wind was waft.

And at the same time by ill hap there fell
  Another arrow out of Cupid's quiver;
The which was carried by the wind at will,
  And under Death the amorous shaft did shiver.
    They being parted, Love took up Death's dart,
    And Death took up Love's arrow, for his part.

Thus as they wandered both about the world,
  At last Death met with one of feeble age;
Wherewith he drew a shaft and at him hurled
  The unknown arrow, with a furious rage,
    Thinking to strike him dead with Death's black dart,
    But he (alas) with Love did wound his heart.

This was the doting fool, this was the man
    That loved fair Gwendolena Queen of Beauty.
She cannot shake him off, do what she can,
    For she hath vowed to her his soul's last duty,
        Making him trim upon the holy-days,
        And crowns his love with garlands made of bays.

Now doth he stroke his beard, and now (again)
    He wipes the drivel from his filthy chin;
Now offers he a kiss; but high disdain
    Will not permit her heart to pity him:
        Her heart more hard than adamant or steel,
        Her heart more changeable than Fortune's wheel.

But leave we him in love (up to the ears)
    And tell how Love behaved himself abroad;
Who seeing one that mourned still in tears
    (A young man groaning under love's great load)
        Thinking to ease his burden, rid his pains:
        For men have grief as long as life remains.

Alas the while, that unawares he drew
    The fatal shaft that Death had dropped before;
By which deceit great harm did then issue,
    Staining his face with blood and filthy gore.
        His face, that was to Gwendolen more dear
        Than love of lords, of any lordly peer.

This was that fair and beautiful young man
    Whom Gwendolena so lamented for;
This is that love whom she doth curse and ban,
    Because she doth that dismal chance abhor;
        And if it were not for his mother's sake,
        Even Ganymede himself she would forsake.

Oh would she would forsake my Ganymede,
  Whose sugared love is full of sweet delight,
Upon whose forehead you may plainly read
  Love's pleasure, graved in ivory tablets bright;
    In whose fair eye-balls you may clearly see
    Base love still stained with foul indignity.

Oh would to God he would but pity me,
  That love him more than any mortal wight:
Then he and I with love would soon agree,
  That now cannot abide his suitors' sight.
    Oh would to God (so I might have my fee)
    My lips were honey, and thy mouth a bee.

Then shouldst thou suck my sweet and my fair flower
  That now is ripe and full of honey-berries;
Then would I lead thee to my pleasant bower
  Filled full of grapes, of mulberries, and cherries;
    Then shouldst thou be my wasp or else my bee,
    I would thy hive, and thou my honey be.

I would put amber bracelets on thy wrests,
  Crownets of pearl about thy naked arms;
And when thou sit'st at swilling Bacchus' feasts,
  My lips with charms should save thee from all harms;
    And when in sleep thou took'st thy chiefest pleasure,
    Mine eyes should gaze upon thine eye-lids' treasure.

And every morn by dawning of the day,
  When Phoebus riseth with a blushing face,
Sylvanus' chapel-clerks shall chaunt a lay,
  And play thee hunts-up in thy resting place;
    My cote thy chamber, my bosom thy bed,
    Shall be appointed for thy sleepy head.

And when it pleaseth thee to walk abroad
    (Abroad into the fields to take fresh air),
The meads with Flora's treasure should be strowed
    (The mantled meadows and the fields so fair),
        And by a silver well, with golden sands,
        I'll sit me down, and wash thine ivory hands.

And in the sweltering heat of summer time,
    I would make cabinets for thee, my love:
Sweet-smelling arbours made of eglantine
    Should be thy shrine, and I would be thy dove.
        Cool cabinets of fresh green laurel boughs
        Should shadow us, o'er-set with thick-set yews.

Or if thou list to bathe thy naked limbs
    Within the crystal of a pearl-bright brook,
Paved with the dainty pebbles to the brims,
    Or clear, wherein thyself thyself mayst look,
        We'll go to Ladon, whose still trickling noise
        Will lull thee fast alseep amidst thy joys.

Or if thou'lt go unto the river side
    To angle for the sweet fresh-water fish,
Armed with thy implements that will abside
    (Thy rod, hook, line) to take a dainty dish;
        Thy rods shall be of cane, thy lines of silk,
        Thy hooks of silver, and thy baits of milk.

Or if thou lov'st to hear sweet melody,
    Or pipe a round upon an oaten reed,
Or make thyself glad with some mirthful glee,
    Or play them music whilst thy flock doth feed;
        To Pan's own pipe I'll help my lovely lad,
        Pan's golden pipe which he of Syrinx had.

Or if thou dar'st to climb the highest trees
    For apples, cherries, medlars, pears, or plums,
Nuts, walnuts, filberts, chestnuts, services,
    The hoary peach, when snowy winter comes;
        I have fine orchards full of mellowed fruit,
        Which I will give thee to obtain my suit.

Not proud Alcinous himself can vaunt
    Of goodlier orchards or of braver trees
Than I have planted; yet thou wilt not grant
    My simple suit; but like the honey bees
        Thou suck'st the flower till all the sweet be gone,
        And lov'st me for my coin till I have none.

Leave Gwendolen (sweet-heart). Though she is fair
    Yet is she light; not light in virtue shining,
But light in her behaviour, to impair
    Her honour in her chastity's declining.
        Trust not her tears, for they can wantonise,
        When tears in pearl are trickling from her eyes.

If thou wilt come and dwell with me at home,
    My sheep-cote shall be strowed with new green rushes;
We'll haunt the trembling prickets as they roam
    About the fields, along the hawthorn bushes.
        I have a piebald cur to hunt the hare:
        So we will live with dainty forest fare.

Nay more than this, I have a garden-plot,
    Wherein there wants nor herbs, nor roots, nor flowers
(Flowers to smell, roots to eat, herbs for the pot),
    And dainty shelters where the welkin lowers:
        Sweet-smelling beds of lilies and of roses,
        Which rosemary banks and lavender encloses.

There grows the gillyflower, the mint, the daisy
  (Both red and white), the blue-veined violet;
The purple hyacinth, the spike to please thee;
    The scarlet-dyed carnation bleeding yet;
      The sage, the savory, and sweet marjoram,
      Hyssop, thyme, and eye-bright, good for the blind
        and dumb.

The pink, the primrose, cowslip, and daffadilly,
  The harebell blue, the crimson columbine,
Sage, lettuce, parsley, and the milk-white lily,
  The rose, and speckled flowers called sops-in-wine,
    Fine pretty king-cups, and the yellow boots
    That grows by rivers and by shallow brooks.

And many thousand moe I cannot name
  Of herbs and flowers that in gardens grow
I have for thee; and coneys that be tame,
  Young rabbits, white as swan and black as crow,
    Some speckled here and there with dainty spots;
    And more I have two milch and milk-white goats.

All these, and more, I'll give thee for thy love,
  If these, and more, may tice thy love away.
I have a pigeon-house, in it a dove,
  Which I love more than mortal tongue can say.
    And last of all, I'll give thee a little lamb
    To play withal, new-weaned from her dam.

But if thou wilt not pity my complaint,
  My tears, nor vows, nor oaths, made to thy beauty,
What shall I do? But languish, die, or faint,
  Since thou dost scorn my tears and my soul's duty;
    And tears contemned, vows and oaths must fail,
    For where tears cannot, nothing can prevail.

Compare the love of fair Queen Gwendolin
    With mine, and thou shalt see how she doth love thee:
I love thee for thy qualities divine,
    But she doth love another swain above thee.
        I love thee for thy gifts, she for her pleasure;
        I for thy virtue, she for beauty's treasure.

And always (I am sure) it cannot last,
    But sometime Nature will deny those dimples:
Instead of beauty (when thy blossom's past)
    Thy face will be deformed, full of wrinkles.
        Then she that loved thee for thy beauty's sake,
        When age draws on, they love will soon forsake.

But I that loved thee for thy gifts divine,
    In the December of thy beauty's waning,
Will still admire, with joy, those lovely eyne,
    That now behold me with their beauties baning.
        Though January will never come again,
        Yet April years will come in showers of rain.

When will my May come, that I may embrace thee?
    When will the hour be of my soul's joying?
Why dost thou seek in mirth still to disgrace me?
    Whose mirth's my health, whose grief's my heart's
        annoying.
        Thy bane my bale, thy bliss my blessedness,
        Thy ill my hell, thy weal my welfare is.

Thus do I honour thee that love thee so,
    And love thee so, that so do honour thee
Much more than any mortal man doth know
    Or can discern by love or jealousy.
        But if that thou disdain'st my loving ever,
        Oh happy I, if I had loved never.

WALT WHITMAN

from Calamus

In paths untrodden,
In the growth by margins of pond-waters,
Escaped from the life that exhibits itself,
From all the standards hitherto publish'd, from the pleasures,
    profits, conformities,
Which too long I was offering to feed my soul,
Clear to me now standards not yet publish'd, clear to me that
    my soul,
That the soul of the man I speak for rejoices in comrades,
Here by myself away from the clank of the world,
Tallying and talk'd to here by tongues aromatic,
No longer abash'd, (for in this secluded spot I can respond
    as I would not dare elsewhere,)
Strong upon me the life that does not exhibit itself,
    yet contains all the rest,
Resolv'd to sing no songs today but those of manly attachment,
Projecting them along that substantial life,
Bequeathing hence types of athletic love,
Afternoon this delicious Ninth-month in my forty-first year,
I proceed for all who are or have been young men,
To tell the secret of my nights and days,
To celebrate the need of comrades.

WALT WHITMAN

from Calamus

When I heard at the close of the day how my name had been
    receiv'd with plaudits in the capitol, still it was not a happy
    night for me that follow'd,
And else when I carous'd, or when my plans were accomplish'd,
    still I was not happy,
But the day when I rose at dawn from the bed of perfect
    health, refresh'd, singing, inhaling the ripe breath of
    autumn,
When I saw the full moon in the west grow pale and disappear
    in the morning light,
When I wander'd alone over the beach, and undressing bathed,
    laughing with the cool waters, and saw the sun rise,
And when I thought how my dear friend my lover was on his
    way coming, O then I was happy,
O then each breath tasted sweeter, and all that day my food
    nourish'd me more, and the beautiful day pass'd well,
And the next came with equal joy, and with the next at evening
    came my friend,
And that night while all was still I heard the waters roll slowly
    continually up the shores,
I heard the hissing rustle of the liquid and sands as directed to
    me whispering to congratulate me,
For the one I love most lay sleeping by me under the same
    cover in the cool night,
In the stillness in the autumn moonbeams his face was inclined
    toward me,
And his arm lay lightly around my breast – and that night
    I was happy.

JOHN ADDINGTON SYMONDS

from Ithocles

That night, when storms were spent and tranquil heaven,
Clear-eyed with stars and fragrant with fresh air,
Slept after thunder, came a sound of song,
And a keen voice that through the forest cried
On Ithocles, and still on Ithocles,
Persistent, till the woods and caverns rang.
He in his lair close-lying and tear-tired
Heard, knew the cry, and trembled. Nearer still
And nearer vibrated the single sound.
Yet, though much called for, Ithocles abode
Prone, deeming that the gods had heard his prayer,
And spake not. Till at the cave-door there stayed
The feet of him who one month since had trodden
Toward that path beneath another moon,
Then Ithocles, thick-throated, 'Who calls me?'
Cried, knowing well the voice of him who called.
'It is Lysander.' 'If indeed it be he,
Let him forgive; strike deep; I ask no more.
Thy coming, youth, long looked for, sets me free;
For now the storm of love and life is o'er,
And I go conquering and conquered down
To darkness and inevitable doom –
Conquered by Kupris who hath had her will,
But having slain within my soul the sin
That made a desert of her garden-ground.
Live happy in the light of holier Love:
Forget the man who willed thee that great wrong.'
'Nay, not so, Ithocles, if this hold good!
For I have left my kith and kin for thee,
And, pricked by sharp stings of importunate love,

Am come to cure thy hurt and heal thy soul.'
'Can this be true? for I do lie as one
Who long hath ta'en a dark and doleful dream:
Waking he shudders, and dim shadowy shapes
Still threaten and weigh down his labouring soul.'
'Rise, Ithocles, and we will speak of Love;
Fierce-eyed, fire-footed, yet most mild of gods
And musical and holy and serene.
Dear to his spirit are deep-chested sighs,
Pitiful pleadings of woe-wearied men,
And the anguish of unutterable things:
But dearer far when heart with heart is wedded,
Body with body, strength with strength; when passion,
Not raging like wild fire in lustful veins,
But centred in the head and heart, doth steady
Twin wills and wishes to a lofty end.
I come to save thee, Ithocles, or die:
Better is death than shame or loveless life.
I love thee as I love this land we tread,
This dear land of our fathers and our gods;
I love thee as I love the light of heaven
Or the sweet life that nourisheth my soul;
Nay, better than all these I love thee, friend;
And wouldst thou have me die, dishonoured die,
In the fair blossom of my April days,
Disconsolate and disinherited,
With all my hopes and happiness undone?'
'What will men say, Lysander, if we love?'
'Let men say what they will. Let us be pure
And faithful to each other to the end.
Life is above and round us, and her dome
Is studded thick with stars of noble deeds,
Each one of which with undivided will
And married purpose we may make our own.
Nay, rise: stand with me at the cavern door:
The storms are over and the skies are clear,

Trembling with dew and moonlight and still stars.
Heaven hears us and the palpitating air,
The woods that murmur, and the streams that leap
Regenerate with tempest-scattered tears;
Be these our temple and our witnesses,
Our idol, altar, oracle, and priest,
Our hymeneal chaunt and holy rite: –
What better need we? and before we die,
All Crete shall bless the marriage of tonight.'

OSCAR WILDE

from Charmides

Down the steep rock with hurried feet and fast
    Clomb the brave lad, and reached the cave of Pan,
And heard the goat-foot snoring as he passed,
    And leapt upon a grassy knoll and ran
Like a young fawn unto an olive wood
Which in a shady valley by the well-built city stood;

And sought a little stream, which well he knew,
    For oftentimes with boyish careless shout
The green and crested grebe he would pursue,
    Or snare in woven net the silver trout,
And down amid the startled reeds he lay
Panting in breathless sweet affright, and waited for the day.

On the green bank he lay, and let one hand
    Dip in the cool dark eddies listlessly,
And soon the breath of morning came and fanned
    His hot flushed cheeks, or lifted wantonly
The tangled curls from off his forehead, while
He on the running water gazed with strange and secret smile.

And soon the shepherd in rough woollen cloak
    With his long crook undid the wattled cotes,
And from the stack a thin blue wreath of smoke
    Curled through the air across the ripening oats,
And on the hill the yellow house-dog bayed
As through the crisp and rustling fern the heavy cattle strayed.

And when the light-foot mower went afield
    Across the meadows laced with threaded dew,
And the sheep bleated on the misty weald,
    And from its nest the waking corncrake flew,
Some woodmen saw him lying by the stream
And marvelled much that any lad so beautiful could seem,

Nor deemed him born of mortals, and one said,
    'It is young Hylas, that false runaway
Who with a Naiad now would make his bed
    Forgetting Herakles,' but others, 'Nay,
It is Narcissus, his own paramour,
Those are the fond and crimson lips no woman can allure.'

And when they nearer came a third one cried,
    'It is young Dionysos who has hid
His spear and fawnskin by the river side
    Weary of hunting with the Bassarid,
And wise indeed were we away to fly:
They live not long who on the gods immortal come to spy.'

[145–186]

FRANCIS KING

Holiday

Two beds, one stripped and one on which I lie.
Hearing the rush of wind, the rasp of rain,
And hither, thither, one small fretful fly,
And high above my head that darkening stain.

The stain spreads out and out. This storm will last
All through the night. The frenzied water slaps
The marble quay, from which no boat is cast.
Mist makes the mountain crumble and collapse.

Below, four figures huddle round a table,
The boatman ponders, then flings down his cards,
As though in some remote, Illyrian fable
A god-man scatters divinatory shards.

What does he read from them? A queasy tossing
Of wave on wave on wave, a thread tugged tight,
Then snapping, as the small boat braves the crossing
Out of this dark into a blaze of light?

The boatman smiles, while in my room above
A vision flickers of those spilled cards lying
Beneath a brutal hand; and all my love
Becomes a long-drawn agony of dying.

ROGER FINCH

The Rape of Ganymede

By eagle's eye, the pubescence on the boy
      is visible as short gold wires. Zeus behind the eye
        sees millions of cells, each cell
      containing a yolk of energy.
      Just as the aggie is about to shoot
from the forefinger fold in front of the boy's thumb,
scattering reds, blues, and greens out of the ring,
      the gate of Heaven rattles its gongs
and Zeus descends the sky on a staircase of wings.

The boy is startled. His playmate, a cousin, runs.
      Later, the cousin will tell that the sea
        fell from the sky, the black waves on fire
      from core to snow-cap, the hammering
      against the air like the hammering of hands
against the heart. He does not understand love,
does not know why his friend did not thrust the flood
      away but stood dancing in it, a god
taking place in him as the sky danced in his blood.

His words will serve as sketch for workers in stone.
      One will show a teenage boy at play
        with an eagle, one will show the bird
      lifting the boy, lifting its quarry.
      Stone cannot hold such motion. Only sound,
the rumblings in the lower strings, the troughs and crests
in the clarinets, the flutes high, high overhead,
      can portray the pair whirling out loud
as they bypass the cousin, arms and wings spread.

GREGORY WOODS

'A goatboy pissing ...'

A goatboy pissing
between roots, sweet vapour
of urine and pine,

turns to me grinning
still pissing, barefoot
in heat of wet needles,

back to his careless herd.
By way of introduction
we gossip soccer

and he goes on and on
naming English teams
as I go down on him.

II STREET LIFE

These are poems which, even if not literally of the streets, nevertheless belong in identifiably urban contexts. Despite the attractions of even a shepherdless rural existence, gay culture has always tended to colonize city spaces and gay poets to claim and name their chosen places. These are usually very specific: Venice (Platen-Hallermünde), Alexandria (Cavafy), Edinburgh (Owen), Rome (Penna), Glasgow (Morgan), San Francisco (Gunn), New York (Ash) and of course London (Stevenson, Treby, Daniels, Kinloch, Johnson). Within the cities, several of these poems record incidents and encounters on buses or trains: to be on the move, it seems, is our natural and necessary state.

There are various implied continuities here, and I've also included two poems – by William Plomer and James Kirkup – which are explicitly meant as homages to C.P. Cavafy and Sandro Penna, whose poems immediately precede them. At the end are two recent poems from Toronto and New York, by R.M. Vaughan and Lawrence Schimel, which offer rather different perspectives on urban gay life: one ruefully funny, the other whimsically domestic.

AUGUST GRAF VON PLATEN-HALLERMÜNDE
Translated by Edwin Morgan

Venetian Sonnets: XII

I love you, as the sum of all those forms
Which Venice in its paintings shows to us.
The very heart may yearn, 'Come close to us!'
But they stand silent, we pass by their charms.

I see you are the breathing stone whose arms
Hold beauty carved for ever motionless.
Pygmalion's rage is still. Victorious
I cannot be, but yours, yours through all storms.

You are a child of Venice, you live here
And stay here; this place is your paradise,
With all Bellini's angels flocking near.

But I – as I glide on, I recognise
I am cheated of a world so great and so dear;
Like the dreams of darkness it dissolves and flies.

WALT WHITMAN

from Calamus

City of orgies, walks and joys,
City whom that I have lived and sung in your midst
    will one day make you illustrious,
Not the pageants of you, not your shifting tableaus,
    your spectacles, repay me,
Not the interminable rows of your houses, nor the ships
    at the wharves,
Nor the processions in the streets, nor the bright windows
    with goods in them,
Nor to converse with learn'd persons, or bear my share
    in the soirée or feast;
Not those, but as I pass O Manhattan, your frequent
    and swift flash of eyes offering me love,
Offering response to my own – these repay me,
Lovers, continual lovers, only repay me.

JOHN GAMBRIL NICHOLSON

Your City Cousins

As I go down the street
A hundred boys a day I meet,
And gazing from my window high
I like to watch them passing by.

I like the boy that earns his bread;
The boy that holds the horse's head,
The boy that tidies up the bar,
The boy that hawks the *Globe* and *Star*.

Smart-looking lads are in my line;
The lad that gives my boots a shine,
The lad that works the lift below,
The lad that's lettered GPO.

I like the boy of business air
That guards the loaded van with care,
Or cycles through the city crowd,
Or adds the ledger up aloud.

I like the boy that's fond of play;
The office-boy cracks jokes all day,
The barber's prentice makes me laugh,
The bookstall-boy gives back my chaff.

When travelling home by tram or train
I meet a hundred boys again,
Behind them on the 'bus I ride
Or pace the platform by their side.

And though I never see you there
All boys your name and nature share,
And almost every day I make
Some new acquaintance for your sake.

C. P. CAVAFY

Translated by John Mavrogordato

The Next Table

He must be hardly twenty-two. And yet
I'm sure that nearly as many years ago
That was the very body I enjoyed.

It isn't a kindling of desire at all.
I only came into the casino a minute ago;
I haven't even had time to drink much.
That very same body I have enjoyed.

If I don't remember where – one thing forgotten doesn't
    signify.

There, now that he has sat down at the next table,
I know every movement he makes – and under his clothes
Naked I can see again the limbs I loved.

WILLIAM PLOMER

A Casual Encounter
In memory of Cavafy, 1863–1933

They met, as most these days do,
among streets, not under leaves; at night;
by what is called chance, some think
predestined; in a capital city, latish;
instantly understanding, without words,
without furtiveness, without guilt,
each had been, without calculation, singled out.

Wherever it was they had met,
without introduction, before drifting this way,
beneath lamps hung high, casting
cones of radiance, hazed with pale dust,
a dry pollenous mist that made
each warm surface seem suede, the sense of touch
sang like a harp; the two were alone.

To be private in public added oddness,
out of doors in a city with millions
still awake, with the heard obbligato
of traffic, that resolute drone,
islanding both, their destination
the shadow they stood in. The place
should perhaps be defined.

But need it? Cliff walls of warehouses;
no thoroughfare; at the end a hurrying
river, dragonish; steel gates locked;
emptiness. Whatever they said
was said gently, was not written down,
not recorded. Neither had need
even to know the other one's name.

Nor do you need to know any more
of an hour so far off, so far,
it may be, from what turns you on.
They, with peacefullest smiles at a rare
Befriedigung, parted, breathing the gold-
dusted, denatured air like the pure
air of some alp: nor met ever again.

Is that all? To you it may seem
a commonplace episode. Once was a man
who might not have thought so. To him
(an old photograph hides his neck clamped
in a high stiff white collar, on his pale face
a false-looking moustache) let me dedicate
this moth-winged encounter, to Cavafy himself.

WILFRED OWEN

Six o'clock in Princes Street

In twos and threes, they have not far to roam,
    Crowds that thread eastward, gay of eyes;
Those seek no further than their quiet home,
    Wives, walking westward, slow and wise.

Neither should I go fooling over clouds,
    Following gleams unsafe, untrue,
And tiring after beauty through star-crowds,
    Dared I go side by side with you;

Or be you in the gutter where you stand,
    Pale rain-flawed phantom of the place,
With news of all the nations in your hand,
    And all their sorrows in your face.

SANDRO PENNA

Translated by Blake Robinson

'I lose myself ... '

I lose myself on a working-class block,
so very busy when evening is near.
For I'm among men quite distant from me,
marvellous men to my eye: radiant,
clear, not known quantities at all.
All the same and unknown and new.

I take the seat, that's in a dark corner,
a worker cedes to me. He chases
after (just making it) a bus in flight.
I didn't see his face, but now
I have his quick-limbed way in my heart.
Left me in that dark corner is what
I took from life – from him, an unknown –
his honest animal smell, like mine.

JAMES KIRKUP

Homo in Omnibus

In memory of Sandro Penna

The rush hour in Naples
lasts all day long, and
most of the night.

In the crowded bus,
the summer suffocated.
I tried to sublimate my agony

by gazing on a boy's delightful face
just out of reach, not out of mind –
that pure smile, those furry eyelashes!

While contemplating that *amour de tête*,
I gradually became aware
of a concern more close –

indeed, right behind me
an urgent male body pressing
with a policeman's truncheon.

I dared not look behind –
indeed I could not, my shoulders pinned –
but I could just insinuate my hand around

against the rough, worn cloth of someone's
cheap cotton working trousers
with its pocketful of change.

Not small change, either,
but something beyond price. I, too,
found myself in a manly condition

(as Nabokov puts its somewhere).
To be the possessor of such riches
in such a humble purse!

At Mergellina, I had to push my way
off the bus – and I was glad to find
he still was pushing close behind me.

On the station escalators,
I finally dared look round – and you
were there. You might have been

anybody, so ordinary did you look.
But you were laughing as your hand outlined
what I was now quite familiar with.

A few words, a handclasp, an offered
cigarette (refused), an arm in mine –
so we prolonged that first encounter,

so dangerously public, in hallowed privacy,
all night together in the small hotel he knew
near Napoli Piazza Garibaldi Termini.

It was an eternal one-night stand,
a passing need, and none the worse for that.
But I have not forgotten our delight.

– And to my surprise, the hotel's name
was 'Sayonara' – a fitting one for a brief
encounter started between two stops.

EDWIN MORGAN

Christmas Eve

Loneliness of city Christmas Eves –
with real stars up there – clear – and stars
on poles and wires across the street, and streaming
cars all dark with parcels, home
to families and the lighted window trees –

I sat down in the bus beside him – white jeans,
black jerkin, slumped with head nodding
in sleep, face hidden by long black hair, hands
tattooed on the four fingers ADEN 1967
and on the right hand five Christian crosses.
As the bus jerked, his hand fell on my knee,
stayed there, lay heavily and alive
with blue carvings from another world
and seemed to hold me like a claw,
unmoving. It moved. I rubbed my ear
to steal a glance at him, found him
stealing a glance at me. It was not
the jerking of the bus, it was a proposition.
He shook his hair back, and I saw his face
for the first time, unshaven, hardman, a warning
whether in Aden or Glasgow, but our eyes held
while that blue hand burned into my leg.
Half drunk, half sleeping – but half what, half what?
As his hand stirred again, my arm covered it
while the bus jolted round a corner.
'Don't ge' aff tae ah ge' aff.' – But the conductor
was watching, came up and shook him, looked at me.
My ticket was up, I had to leave him sprawled there
with that hand that now seemed so defenceless

lying on the seat I had left. Half down the stair
I looked back. The last thing I saw was Aden
and five blue crosses for five dead friends.

It was only fifteen minutes out of life
but I feel as if I was lifted by a whirlwind
and thrown down on some desert rocks to die
of dangers as always far worse lost than run.

FRANCIS KING

The Address

I did not think that I would care
    After that last shrugged-off caress
That I should still be here, he there,
    The distance might be more or less
And more or less my brief despair,
    When I was given that address.

I did not think that I would lie
    Upon the grass where we had lain,
Willing upon the vacant eye
    A face I would not see again –
A face beneath that foreign sky
    Which now could only bring me pain.

I did not think that I would take
    Train, bus and mule to find that spot,
Sealed in the hills beside a lake,
    Where everything was green with rot;
But otherwise how could I break
    That odd and unrelenting knot?

I did not think I'd care at all,
    Being so tricked, but none the less
My body ached as from a fall.
    Strange that the cause of my distress
Should be a thing so very small –
    A false address, a false address.

THOM GUNN

San Francisco Streets

I've had my eye on you
    For some time now.
You're getting by it seems,
    Not quite sure how.
But as you go along
    You're finding out
What different city streets
    Are all about.

Peach country was your home.
    When you went picking
You ended every day
    With peach fuzz sticking
All over face and arms,
    Intimate, gross,
Itching like family,
    And far too close.

But when you came to town
    And when you first
Hung out on Market Street
    That was the worst:
Tough little group of boys
    Outside Flagg's Shoes.
You learned to keep your cash.
    You got tattoos.

Then by degrees you rose
    Like country cream –
Hustler to towel boy,

Bath house and steam;
Tried being kept a while –
      But felt confined,
One brass bed driving you
      Out of your mind.

Later on Castro Street
      You got new work
Selling chic jewelry.
      And as sales clerk
You have at last attained
      To middle class.
(No one on Castro Street
      Peddles his ass.)

You gaze out from the store.
      Watching you watch
All the men strolling by
      I think I catch
Half-veiled uncertainty
      In your expression.
Good looks and great physiques
      Pass in procession.

You've risen up this high –
      How, you're not sure.
Better remember what
      Makes you secure.
Fuzz is still on the peach,
      Peach on the stem.
Your looks looked after you.
      Look after them.

QUENTIN STEVENSON

Hampstead Notebook:
The Boy with the Broken Arm

Chin raised
he breathes through closed eyelids
and the upper lip tightens
with the delicate old man tremors
of a face reaching for sun.

Canine clamped
to the nail on the index finger of his left hand
the arm trailing

while the other
in its loser's cast
not one signature offered or asked for
a month's shame in the white
beats time on his belly
to the music of whatever makes him smile.

Blue tattoo
which tonight he'll need to wash off
clematis also blue.

He likes the angle of his crossed leg
the first chafing of sweat
the heat trapped in his crutch.

But now he would like without opening his eyes
to undress.
The man who has passed three times
and stopped once
will not go on waiting.

Well here I am.
But do not expect me to look at you.
I'm different.
And mad.
I spoil things.
Everything about me is wrong.

IVOR C. TREBY

Incident on the Central Line

you zipped up too fast when the train came in
reluctant to stop you left it too late
there under the arches at Lancaster Gate
the metal teeth bit through the foreskin

i stood and watched through the tubetrain door
as you your game with the other forsook
saw your whitening face and your stricken look
the bright line of blood on the floor

three nights later the dried stains bear
witness a moment you'll not soon forget
i see your face when these drops were wet
and the smile that even then lingered there

PETER DANIELS

Liverpool St

Meeting without meaning to, crossing the marble floors
of the refurbished terminus, we celebrate with food, choosing
station pastries or cartons of burger-fries; and we talk
on the train, or sometimes we don't; sometimes that matters,
for reasons of living together, making our way home.

Tonight on the five-forty-five, the couple sitting opposite
get working on separate crosswords, like in-trays of invoices,
till one anagram calls out for the full attention of two;
and silently they distribute all of the concatenations,
finding between them the unspoken words to balance the
        clues.

Catching up with each other halfway to where we're going
any day is a likelihood, and an unexpected extra.
We meet in a station, or we coincide in the bathroom,
we cross and merge in parallels less than a pillow apart:
joined-up people, finding the world as wide as our bed.

JOHN ASH

Following a Man

I was following a man
with a handsome, intelligent face
(the cheekbones high, the nose straight, the lips
sufficiently full), and judging by the shape
of his neck (an unfailingly reliable
indicator in my experience) a lithe, athletic
figure; or, to be more exact, he and I were merely walking
in the same direction along Seventh Avenue,
having earlier stood side by side in the Old Chelsea Post Office:
the day was Friday, June 9th, the time late afternoon,
and after only two or three blocks,
each full of particular events and distractions
(such as dogs, clouds, paupers, hydrants, hairdressers),
I began to feel that I was almost in love with this man,
that, like a song, I would follow him anywhere ...

Something about the way he slicked back his hair
delighted me, and I admired his beautiful raincoat
which so enhanced the easy masculine grace
of his movements. I was concentrating hard,
trying to take in all these details without giving
any cause for embarrassment (either on my part
or his) when he swerved into a newspaper store
between 16th Street and 15th, and I could think of no
plausible excuse for following him into that meagre space
where, surely, our eyes would have been forced to meet,
and I would have blushed (he being protected by a light tan).

In all likelihood he is lost to me, as
he would have been had that door been
the door to an elevator in an apartment building
bigger than all the pyramids combined.
Even if he should prove to be my near-neighbour
I doubt that I will ever see him again,
since in New York there are always too many
neighbours to keep track of (you hear
their footsteps, their voices and their music,
but it is difficult to attach these attributes
to a particular person, in much the same way
that an archaeologist may uncover the fragments
of a mirror but will never know the face
that, day by day, was reflected there)
but it is not as if he were dead. He exists
and will continue to do so for some time, perhaps
for many years, and as I walked without hesitation
directly past the store he had entered I was overcome
with a sudden feeling of elation at the thought
that it was within my power to record this incident
which is unexceptional
as the budding of pear trees in their season,
unrepeatable as the first sight of a great city.

STEPHEN TAPSCOTT

The Queens

One queen squeals as the other retreats,
flings a drink after him overhand,
baptizing the bystanders, making a scene
the two apparently need to create:

some hissy diva-drama, obscure and public.
And I'm soaked. Even my socks (a last-minute gift
from M. at the airport, saying *take care of
yourself*, meaning *I can't say this,*

I can hardly stand this) and suddenly
I'm standing in a bog. What am I
supposed to do? Do I squeal too? I
don't owe them that. Do I laugh benignly,

as if this whole embarrassing business
were funny, were my idea of fun?
Do I smile knowingly (the Older Man,
wiser and gentler, in expensive shoes)?

Or suck in my belly and scowl (*yes Daddy*)?
Or stick out my belly and growl at some kid
(*please Master*) as if he were to blame for it?
None of these options feels like freedom, exactly.

The flannel-plaids and sleeveless vests
settle for a shrug, a side-long chuckle,
a manlier grip on their beer-bottles
... and the tide subsides. Two college sweatshirts

boogy in place, locating each other
by echo. I'm getting too old for this.
I know why M. needs it – the practice,
the disco, the visual flick of desire,

the shock of being wanted: because it is difficult
and possible; because a young gay man
needs to be given, over and over, permission
to need; because he is handsome and he feels

darkly that somehow this affects his life,
not yet that beauty like his is a gift
to console him for his youth. He is young
and will be hurt, and hurt others, in time.

– because having grown up in this culture
a man has passed the standard social rites
and needs to return, to do it right
the second round, to learn the rules of pleasure

and honesty, party-behaviour and sweet
repression, as a queer and decent man.
It's a funny business, this sex thing,
so thorough and so incomplete. The queens

are dancing now, shirtless, rolling their waists,
and their solitude is terrifying. They enact
for us something more rooted than politics,
or privacy: that we are people, an 'us',

a community … but of what? shared need? Can
such affection matter, if we offer it
beyond persons – to any hunky trick,
or to men collectively, or to some man,

lucky particular, who summarizes
for the moment what one seems to want

for the moment, for the empty weekend?
Is this display itself a kind of tie,

an icon of raw want? A community,
what is that? Do I mean a collection
of the brave and the needy, of whom
these feral dancing boys,

posing and turning in the hard music,
are our ambassadors, shamans, poets?
Maybe I'd explain it that way to some judge
who stood beyond the threshold of the subject.

[Note to myself, for future sonnet:
embarrassment: a form of jealousy;
implies the judgement of an uninvolved
third party; not shame; laughs-with? Develop.]

This scrimmage of allegiance and resistance,
I wonder how it differs from any other
citizenship a grown man chooses. These are
my people. We danced together into the camps.

And yet we embarrass me, and squeal,
and pour beer in my favourite socks. These years,
anyone can die of misjudged sex:
we know, we all

know. And know too a man can wear away
from solitude: no one is immune.
How can I be too proud to be here,
when I feel the same urgency

that moves them, dancing? Shocked by joy, to see
in the torque of that long boy's waist the same
white turning as M.'s, his torso, when he winds
a towel around himself, so pure it sears me.

The symmetry of it: we are one body and are
each apart. Though whether this lurching fugue
of sex and its pulses are the effect
or the fact of the loneliness, curse

or the first cure, whether this dancing
exposing their waists can make them happy
(as I am for the moment, liftingly happy),
who am I to say for them? I can say

we are a people, whatever that signifies
in language or in longing, or in belonging
exactly through this pulse and its common
motions, or through this saying, obliquely

for us all. The queens are lofting, angelic
now. The T-shirt with the kind moustache
has asked the skinny overalls to dance
(as he had hoped there shyly, glancing);

Big Daddy (even his cigar is leather) is buzzing
over the boy in the wire-rimmed glasses,
they sway as the sinuous music passes
through them, they are discussing

insect-images of sexuality in Proust ... We
are one body; we lift and embarrass me –
and I'm grateful, I realize, may be
for that most of all –: we amuse me,

in the vast implausible surprise
of being here ... though it's getting loud
in this blue cellar; it's late; it's packed; the crowd
is turning younger, and the hot smoke burns my eyes.

PAUL WILKINS

My Tired Darlings

My tired darlings, with what swift
tact they leave before it's light.
Their January steps crack ice, the clear glass
breaks to webs; my darlings pace to

families, overdrafts, subtleties.
They wake to noon in their beds,
thinking through speeches that for them
are regret or revenge or that one long truth.

They work in bars, in whitewashed attics
they suck at their smoking lives,
they talk of their children who need them more,
they press hands flat across aching eyes.

Their explanations to tomorrow
flicker in their throats like injured things.
They have to get back, my tired darlings;
they are wanting to be elsewhere and themselves.

Their tongues flick swiftly across upper lips,
tasting what hasn't happened.
You can imagine it, it's on a Tuesday,
there's no one who knows.

They don't want much of this, my darlings,
but tired white fleshes lie down again,
fat candles blub their wax, a voice is dressing afterwards
and murmuring the number of a cab-firm.

I love them, their moments of winning,
thinking they choose their havens and departures.
Knowing the long world wants them for its own,
they pat their pockets for keys, small change.

MARC ALMOND

The Puerto Rican GoGo Boy

The Puerto Rican gogo boy
Gyrates in front of me,
Hard body of the slums,
Hard mind of the street.
He has his two front teeth missing,
When he grins
His face resembles a splintered fence.
He has spots on his cheeks
Dope in his eyes
Murder on his fingers
(Not in his heart)
Only 'mom' in his heart.
On his shoulder a purple sore
That draws me in
Fascinated:
On his forearm his true
Love etched into his flesh
With a rusty switch
He thrusts
And his cock bounces joyfully
Against the satin finish
Of his black Adidas shorts,
To the muffled disco beat
He strips,
And grins
And you've just got to love him.
And he juts his hips towards you,
A five dollar bill tucked into the elastic waistband
Of his black Adidas shorts:
Bringing you a Latin word of love in your ear

And perhaps a sloppy kiss if you're over forty
And loaded:
It worries me,
I got a sloppy kiss, the word of love.
He sits
Legs apart on a small stool
To remove his cheap trainers,
His grubby white socks.
He grins and rubs his crotch,
The over forties go wild
With the five dollar bills.
He removes his shorts,
His dick is average
And refuses to harden,
He tugs it, twangs it
Pulls it and pummels it:
It died!
The (lucky) few at the front
Get to gum it,
Slurping and spitting it.
The Puerto Rican gogo boy dances on
To 'Call Me' by Blondie,
To 'Disco Inferno' by the Tramps.
I follow the tracks up his arms
To gaze at the purple sore.
The torso a tight washboard,
A steaming ploughed farm field;
The muscles gold and defiant.
He loves his work.
Afterwards ten dollars buys you a private show.
His name is Roberto.

DAVID KINLOCH

In Brompton Cemetery

Quiet seeps in
on the bellied drone
of planes.

A patter of squirrel
feet fall like rain
across the tombs

and spirit my
glance to *Prince
Bibesco*. Moss

unletters his name;
so many half-
caught: *widow*

of, infant, dearly.
Grass ears fritter
away and offer

occasional unknown
wild-flowers, the
tangled dark

at the bole of trees,
half a bench
fraying into shadow.

Pigeons examining
my feet are far
from ghosts

and only Richard
Tauber's grave
sings against

forgetfulness,
bedecked in pansies,
the high C of a single

iris. Lichens
resist each note
we strike here,

the true tenor of it:
just web and brief
silver, the beaten body

of the earth.

A strafe of
melon seeds
pave you to the picket

fence of a white
quiet canton
and the RIP boys

aged 21 or 23 who
served, defended, rest.
Other ones pad by

outside in designer
names that flare
the cemetery blur,

ignite the spokes
of lycrad cyclers
who lap them, alight

among unconsecrated
colonnades and await
the tryst. Pot-bellies

amble their desire
among the athletes
and there the game

of seek and seek
begins: a lithe
of muscle suns

its walkman on
a slab: his silver
shades annealed

like salamanders
to his eyes.
A hot wind uplifts

choruses of stares
across the unkempt
stones and all aches

to be fenced
in a corner, asked
for a momentary

name. A little blond
manfully defends
his plot, watches

the slow summer-
stunned bee crash
the asphalt, shed

a wing and wipe its eyes.

JOEL LANE

The Outline of a House

It's safe, you say, nobody walks
through here. It's not a street any more,
just a blind alley. At this corner

they're demolishing a house. But nobody
works at this time of night. Follow
me through the scaffolding. This way.

This was a bed, it could have been
our bed – this paved rectangle
between a shallow trench and a wall.

This was someone's roof, this brick height
that nurtures a bleached flower, while
stars hang like pollen in a distant shaft.

Crouching, you pull me down to the pavement
like a condemned building. I lift you
until your filament burns itself out

and a shattered moth flies to the dust.
We are holding each other. This
is home. We can leave it behind.

STEVE ANTHONY

Life Drawing
for Clive

If we'd been straight, coming out
of our station off the last train,
you wouldn't have noted the fit of my jeans
as I pushed through the ticket barrier.
I might not have seen the small red pin
on the charcoal lapel of your overcoat;

you wouldn't have shot me a look
among the late suburban stragglers,
and I definitely wouldn't have followed,
paused, followed you down that dark alley
where you'd stopped for a piss (you smiled
Got a light? – of course, I carry matches);

I'd never have kissed you, fallen to my knees
in the bushes, your belt buckle clanking
as somebody passed only feet away;
I wouldn't have walked you home by the lake
where the moon made pearls of the sleeping geese
and a screech owl drew us closer.

And maybe if we hadn't done all of this,
though we never did turn into lovers,
we'd have missed this other sharing –
talking through lines of Gunn or Hockney
as you sketch me on your bed,
my only prop a finger of whisky.

ADAM JOHNSON

Early November

The day was gold early and I went out under the wind
Over the vivid leaves as they were singing in whispers –
A high day with a blue brim riding the roof-backs,
Leaving the trees red in amazement at their own brightness.
Down Piccadilly to the Circus on a sleak fourteen,
I went, in my long coat, into the heart of town,
Alighted, danced with several people, kissed one I knew
Whose cheek was blushed with cold, called at a bar in
        Poland Street,
And overheard the discourse of a dozen thirsty souls.

The day was cold early and I went back in sudden rain
Under lamps, by windows flushed with light in upper rooms,
Among people dancing out of offices and stores
Into the brilliant streets and the cool ballroom of evening,
Over the dark-drowned leaves that were singing in whispers.

10 Reasons Why I Fall in Love with Inaccessible Straight Boys Every Damn Time

1. cause when he laughs at my jokes or tells me he likes my clothes it can't be anything but the truth.

2. straight boys speak a foreign tongue I never learned – a semaphore of scruffy chin tugs, bearish shoulders, and dead dog easy posture, straight boys can spit, far, and seem to like urinals.

3. a straight boy will always hate opera and will never, ever play some god-awful Whitney Houston record before he feels you up on the couch – straight boys like guitars.

4. cause foreign films are for girls with glasses or nervous Anglican boys who went to private school – and Yes, Thank You, he does eat meat.

5. straight boys don't trust their fathers either.

6. a straight boy will wear a tight T-shirt no matter how fat he is. I call this Innocence.

7. OK, yes, even if does have three kids and two monthly car payments and at least one house he still has more money than most of the fags I know and Money = Relaxation.

8. cause once I went to the Y and I swear to God four straight boys massaged each other buck naked and talked about body fat ratios and not one got hard or even a little glassy-eyed and I knew, I knew I was on another planet and I have always wanted to see the stars up close.

9. straight boys remind me of children – big, hapless, grown-up children with sex organs it would be right and legal and far more interesting to touch.

10. because women don't really trust them, they'd be better off with me.

LAWRENCE SCHIMEL

Using the Poet's Bathroom
for R.H.

      The Greeks were only half correct
that a woman might turn men's flesh hard as stone;
      yours, perhaps, would not grow erect

at the sight of her, but of her own she has
      complete control. Looking inward,
so like mirrors' truths, Maude, too, turned stone: topaz

      gems that floated in her bladder.
You tell this tale to explain why, like a male
      dog, she lifts one leg to splatter

the black plastic sacks of garbage with her scent,
      a splendid anecdote about
your discovery that she was a latent

      hermaphrodite. But there is more
at stake than regaling friends on midnight walks
      with Maude, who had waited hours

for your return without an accident. Such
      is the devotion of women
and dogs; the strength of will to endure so much

      time alone, sustained only by
the idea of commitment to them. Maude
      held tight to her purpose. The gay

man's best friend, it was not in imitative
    flattery she tried to grow a
penis, but because she recognized your love

    of sameness over difference.
A threshold she could not fully cross, her attempts
    at genital enlargements

contradicted your earlier lines: *a choice
    that always, when there is a door,
even a French one, must be made.* Sacrifice

    her identity, though she tried,
Maude was left whining about sex and her
    crepuscular gender, outside

your bathroom door. In that earlier poem,
    Max, too, whined; for both dogs *the word
toilet clearly suggests the twilight, some*

    subliminal ending. They were
restricted to those parlours overflowing
    with your public life, books and art:

needlepoint pugs on pillows, porcelain pugs,
    pugs in every medium, all gifts.
Pigs, too, for they had monopolized your thoughts

    before your vowels lengthened. On
an island of vowels, Odysseus
    had come to know and love swine.

Returned to Ithaca, his sole *memento
    amori* was a piggy bank –
two copulating corpulent pigs into

whose corpulent bellies he dropped coins
for his son's wedding. Only his faithful dog,
        after sniffing at the man's loins,

had recognized him. Though too short to reach
        men's crotches, Maude could smell where your
true affections lay. In your bathroom, where flesh

        is exposed from its civilized
garb, ostensibly free from all onlookers
        except that narcissean gaze,

there is no room for animals. Photographs
        of men cover every surface
(the ceiling even!) as if this were a hive,

        each man locked into his own frame
like a cell of memory's honey, and when
        the shower fills the room with steam

these boys, unlike bees, do not flee. Mentors, friends,
        lovers, the men who have shaped your life,
it was yet too soon to know if I would stand

        among their ranks. I stood before
their ancient glittering eyes and unzipped my
        pants. I could not hope to compare.

III LADS' LOVE

Love poetry – regardless of sexuality – has always had a natural inclination to celebrate the beauty and desirability of subjects who are significantly younger than their admiring authors (also regardless of the fact that the young are ignorant, vain, selfish, unreliable ...). This section includes poems which lament the passing of youth (as the ancient Greeks and Romans almost invariably do); which record the poet's devotion to a younger lover (Shakespeare, Ackerley); or which recall a time, perhaps only the day before yesterday, when both poet and subject were equally youthful – most of the poets towards the end of the chapter were, after all, still in their twenties at the time of writing the poems. It even includes one or two hints about all that ignorance, vanity and so forth.

The longest item here, Richard Essenden's 'Effects', is a beautifully balanced sequence about a man–boy relationship which begins in the author's adolescence and develops into a long-term affair: it is a fitting reminder that while an anthology such as this one may be divided into more or less arbitrary sections, life itself bridges the divisions in sometimes unexpected ways; it is also, I think, a marvellous piece of writing.

SOLON

Translated by J. A. Symonds

'Blest is the man ... '

Blest is the man who loves and after early play
Whereby his limbs are supple made and strong,
Retiring to his house, with wine and song
Toys with a fair boy on his breast the livelong day!

ALCAEUS

Translated by Mark Beech

'You're getting hairy legs ... '

You're getting hairy legs, Nicander;
Soon you'll have a bristly bum.
You'll learn then how lovers become
Scarcer than youth that would not linger.

[*The Greek Anthology*, XII:30]

CATULLUS

Translated by C.H. Sisson

XV

I commend to you myself and my love,
Aurelius, and make a modest request:
If you have known what it is to desire
One whom you wanted left untouched
Then keep this boy untouched for me.
It is not the great world that I fear;
Those who go up and down the street
Are lost in their own preoccupations.
What I fear is you and your penis
Which is after boys, good-looking or not.
Exercise it as much as you like
Out of the house, however you like:
But spare this one, it is little to ask.
If your ill mind and rapacious fury
Carry you on to such a point
That you do not stop at this injury
Then you shall suffer, with feet tied up
And mullet and radishes stuck up your arse.

XLVIII

If I should be allowed to go as far as kissing
Your sweet eyes, Juventius,
I would go on kissing them three hundred thousand times
Nor would it ever seem I had had enough,
Not if I harvested
Kisses as numerous as the ears of standing corn.

XCIX

I kissed you while you were playing, sweet Juventius;
It was sweeter than the sweetest ambrosia.
I did not do it with impunity: for more than an hour,
I remember, it was as if I was hung up on a cross
And I could not talk myself out of it with tears
Or get the slightest reduction of your anger.
As soon as it was done you rinsed your lips with a lot of water
And wiped them with every joint of your fingers
So that nothing contracted from my mouth would remain
As if it were the filthy spit of a dirty whore.

Besides you forthwith handed me over to hostile love
And tortured me in every way
So that from being ambrosia that kiss was changed
Into the sharpest of sharp helllebore.
Since that is the penalty you exact for my unfortunate love
I will never steal kisses from you again.

MARTIAL

Translated by Ian Shelton

Epigram IV.7

How, Hyllus, dare you today deny
What you gave gladly yesterday?
You, who were then so accommodating,
Now obstinately prevaricating!

You mutter about your sprouting hairs,
Your new-grown beard and gathering years:
But just how long must one night be
To create this great maturity?

Why, Hyllus, do you tease me so,
Who loved me a mere day ago?
If then a boy how, without warning,
Have you become a man this morning?

MARTIAL
Translated by Anthony Reid

Epigram XI.8

The breath of balm from foreign branches pressed;
    The effluence that falling saffron brings;
The scent of apples ripening in a chest;
    Or the rich foliage of a field in Spring;

Imperial silken robes from Palatine;
    Or amber, warming in a virgin's hand;
The far-off smell of spilt Falernian wine;
    A bee-loud garden in Sicilian land;

Odour, which spice and altar-incense send;
    Or wreath of flowerets from a rich brow drawn;
Why speak of these? Words fail. Their perfect blend
    Resemble my boy's kiss at early dawn.

You ask his name? Only to kiss him? Well!
You swear as much? Sabinus, I won't tell.

STRATO OF SARDIS

Translated by Mark Beech

'Much as I like ... '

Much as I like a twelve year old's cock,
A thirteen year old's is even better;
Love's sweet flower is fourteen years old,
Yet at just fifteen he'll be still tastier;
Sixteen's for gods, while as for seventeen,
That's Zeus's prerogative. And if you
Want them older, they're no fun –
You're heading after two-way traffic.

[*The Greek Anthology*, XII: 4]

STRATO OF SARDIS

Translated by Mark Beech

'I met a boy ... '

I met a boy among the market-stalls,
Weaving a garland out of berries and petals.
I couldn't pass him by. I hovered there
Until at last I found the chance to whisper:
'How much will it cost me to buy your crown?'
Blushing redder than his roses, staring down,
Under his breath he stammered: 'You must go.
Get out of here before my father sees you.'
I bought some wreaths for form's sake, took them home,
Then crowned the gods and prayed that I may have him.

[*The Greek Anthology*, XII:8]

MICHAEL DRAYTON

from Piers Gaveston

This Edward in the April of his age,
Whilst yet the crown sat on his father's head,
My Jove with me, his Ganymede, his page,
Frolic as May, a lusty life we led:
    He might command, he was my sovereign's son,
    And what I said, by him was ever done.

My words as laws authentic he allowed,
Mine yea, by him was never crossed as no;
All my conceit as currant he avowed,
And as my shadow still he servèd so:
    My hand the racket, he the tennis ball,
    My voice's echo, answering every call.

My youth the glass where he his youth beheld,
Roses his lips, my breath sweet nectar showers,
For in my face was nature's fairest field,
Richly adorned with beauty's rarest flowers.
    My breast his pillow, where he laid his head,
    Mine eyes his book, my bosom was his bed.

My smiles were life, and Heaven unto his sight,
All his delight concluding my desire;
From my sweet sun, he borrowed all his light,
And as a fly played with my beauty's fire.
    His lovesick lips at every kissing qualm,
    Cling to my lips, to cure their grief with balm.

Like as the wanton ivy with his twine,
Whenas the oak his rootless body warms,
The straightest saplings strictly doth combine,
Clipping the woods with his lascivious arms:
    Such our embraces when our sport begins,
    Lapped in our arms, like Leda's lovely twins.

Or as love-nursing Venus when she sports,
With cherry-lipped Adonis in the shade,
Figuring her passions in a thousand sorts,
With sighs, and tears, or what else might persuade,
    Her dear, her sweet, her joy, her life, her love,
    Kissing his brow, his cheek, his hand, his glove.

My beauty was the loadstar of his thought,
My looks the pilot to his wandering eye,
By me his senses all asleep were brought,
When with sweet love I sang his lullaby.
    Nature had taught my tongue her perfect time,
    Which in his ear stroke duly as a chime.

With sweetest speech, thus could I sirenise,
Which as strong filters youth's desire could move,
And with such method could I rhetorise,
My music played the measures to his love:
    In his fair breast, such was my soul's impression,
    As to his eyes, my thoughts made intercession.

Thus like an eagle seated in the sun,
But yet a phoenix in my sovereign's eye,
We act with shame, our revels are begun,
The wise could judge of our catastrophe:
    But we proceed to play our wanton prize,
    Our mournful chorus was a world of eyes.

[211–264]

CHRISTOPHER MARLOWE

from Edward II

Gaveston:
'My father is deceased; come Gaveston,
And share the kingdom with thy dearest friend.'
Ah words that make me surfeit with delight;
What greater bliss can hap to Gaveston
Than live and be the favourite of a king?
Sweet prince I come; these, these thy amorous lines
Might have enforced me to have swum from France.
And like Leander gasped upon the sand,
So thou wouldst smile and take me in thy arms.
The sight of London to my exiled eyes
Is as Elysium to a new-come soul;
Not that I love the city or the men
But that it harbours him I hold so dear,
The king, upon whose bosom let me die
And with the world be still at enmity.
What need the arctic people love starlight,
To whom the sun shines both by day and night?
Farewell base stooping to the lordly peers;
My knee shall bow to none but to the king.
As for the multitude that are but sparks,
Raked up in embers of their poverty,
Tanti; I'll fan first on the wind,
That glanceth at my lips and flieth away.

   [1.1.1–23]

I must have wanton poets, pleasant wits,
Musicians, that with touching of a string
May draw the pliant king which way I please;

Music and poetry is his delight,
Therefore I'll have Italian masques by night,
Sweet speeches, comedies and pleasing shows,
And in the day when he shall walk abroad,
Like sylvan nymphs my pages shall be clad,
My men like satyrs grazing on the lawns
Shall with their goat feet dance an antic hay;
Sometimes a lovely boy in Dian's shape,
With hair that gilds the water as it glides,
Crownets of pearl about his naked arms,
And in his sportful hands an olive-tree
To hide those parts which men delight to see,
Shall bathe him in a spring, and there hard by
One like Actaeon peeping through the grove
Shall by the angry goddess be transformed,
And running in the likeness of an hart,
By yelping hounds pulled down and seem to die;
Such things as these best please his majesty.

[1.1.51–70]

WILLIAM SHAKESPEARE

Sonnet 20

A woman's face, with Nature's own hand painted,
Hast thou, the master mistress of my passion;
A woman's gentle heart, but not acquainted
With shifting change, as is false women's fashion;
An eye more bright than theirs, less false in rolling,
Gilding the object whereupon it gazeth;
A man in hue all hues in his controlling,
Which steals men's eyes and women's souls amazeth.
And for a woman wert thou first created,
Till Nature as she wrought thee fell a-doting,
And by addition me of thee defeated,
By adding one thing to my purpose nothing.
  But since she pricked thee out for women's pleasure,
  Mine be thy love, and thy love's use their treasure.

ROBERT HERRICK

To Music, to becalm a sweet-sick-youth

Charms, that call down the moon from out her sphere,
On this sick youth work your enchantments here:
Bind up his senses with your numbers, so,
As to entrance his pain, or cure his woe.
Fall gently, gently, and a while him keep
Lost in the civil wilderness of sleep:
That done, then let him, dispossess'd of pain,
Like to a slumb'ring bride, awake again.

JOHN WILMOT, EARL OF ROCHESTER

Song

Love a Woman! y'are an Ass,
'Tis a most insipid Passion,
To choose out for your happiness
The silliest part of God's Creation.

Let the Porter, and the Groome,
Things design'd for dirty Slaves,
Drudge in fair *Aurelia*'s Womb,
To get supplies for Age and Graves.

Farewel Woman, I intend,
Henceforth, ev'ry Night to sit,
With my lewd well-natur'd Friend,
Drinking, to engender Wit.

Then give me Health, Wealth, Mirth, and Wine,
And if busie Love intrenches,
There's a sweet soft Page of mine,
Does the trick worth Forty Wenches.

WALT WHITMAN

We Two Boys Together Clinging

We two boys together clinging,
One the other never leaving,
Up and down the roads going, North and South
      excursions making,
Power enjoying, elbows stretching, fingers clutching,
Arm'd and fearless, eating, drinking, sleeping, loving,
No law less than ourselves owning, sailing, soldiering,
      thieving, threatening,
Misers, menials, priests alarming, air breathing, water
      drinking, on the turf or the sea-beach dancing,
Cities wrenching, ease scorning, statues mocking,
      feebleness chasing,
Fulfilling our foray.

GERARD MANLEY HOPKINS

The Bugler's First Communion

A bugler boy from barrack (it is over the hill
There) – boy bugler, born, he tells me, of Irish
    Mother to an English sire (he
Shares the best gifts surely, fall how things will).

This very very day came down to us after a boon he on
My late being there begged of me, overflowing
    Boon in my bestowing,
Came, I say, this day to it – to a First Communion.

Here he knelt then in regimental red.
Forth Christ from cupboard fetched, how fain I of feet
    To his youngster take his treat!
Low latched in leaf light housel his too huge godhead.

There! and your sweetest sendings, ah divine,
By it, heavens, befall him! as a heart Christ's darling, dauntless;
    Tongue true, vaunt- and tauntless;
Breathing bloom of a chastity in mansex fine.

Frowning and forefending angel-warder
Squander the hell-rook ranks sally to molest him;
    March, kind comrade, abreast him;
Dress his days to a dextrous and starlight order.

How it dóes my heart good, visiting us at that bleak hill,
When limber liquid youth, that to all I teach
    Yields tender as a pushed peach,
Hies headstrong to its wellbeing of a self-wise self-will!

Then though I should tread tufts of consolation
Dáys áfter, só I in a sort deserve to
        And do serve God to serve to
Just such slips of soldiery Christ's royal ration.

Nothing élse is like it, no, not all so strains
Us: fresh youth fretted in a bloomfall all portending
        That sweet's sweeter ending;
Realm both Christ is heir to and thére réigns.

O now well work that sealing sacred ointment!
O for now charms, arms, what bans off bad
        And locks love ever in a lad!
Let mé though see no more of him, and not disappointment

Those sweet hopes quell whose least me quickenings lift,
In scarlet or somewhere of some day seeing
        That brow and bead of being,
An our day's God's own Galahad. Though this child's drift

Seems by a divine bloom chánnelled, nor do I cry
Disaster there; but there may he not rankle and roam
        In backwheels though bound home? –
That left to the Lord of the Eucharist, I here lie by;

Recorded only, I have put my lips on pleas
Would brandle adamantine heaven with ride and jar, did
        Prayer go disregarded;
Forward-like, but however, and like favourable heaven heard
        these.

HORATIO BROWN

Bored

At a London Music

Two rows of foolish faces blent
In two blurred lines; the compliment,
The formal smile, the cultured air,
The sense of falseness everywhere.
Her ladyship superbly dressed –
   I liked their footman, John, the best.

The tired musician's ruffled mien,
Their whispered talk behind the screen,
The frigid plaudits, quite confined
By fear of being unrefined.
His lordship's grave and courtly jest –
   I liked their footman, John, the best.

Remote I sat with shaded eyes,
Supreme attention in my guise,
And heard the whole laborious din,
Piano, 'cello, violin;
And so, perhaps, they hardly guessed
   I liked their footman, John, the best.

WILFRED OWEN

To ——

Three rompers run together, hand in hand.
The middle boy stops short, the others hurtle:
What bumps, what shrieks, what laughter turning turtle.
Love, racing between us two, has planned
A sudden mischief: shortly he will stand
And we shall shock. We cannot help but fall;
What matter? Why, it will not hurt at all,
Our youth is supple, and the world is sand.

Better our lips should bruise our eyes, than He,
Rude love, out-run our breath; you pant, and I,
I cannot run much farther; mind that we
Both laugh with love; and having tumbled, try
To go forever children, hand in hand.
The sea is rising ... and the world is sand.

J.R. ACKERLEY

from After the Blitz, 1941

Invocation to a soldier reported missing

Observe! I turn the key in this new door
At which you have not knocked your gay tattoo;
Note the bright prospect down the passage to
The sunlit terrace (this conducted tour

Is specially for you) and disregard
The snake on that far threshold, it's a pigeon
Craning for crumbs; we need no admonition
That life's unstable and our due reward.

But praise me for my courage: could you tell,
Here in the anteroom, here in the parlour,
That all this newly painted furniture
Three months ago was refuse raked from hell?

Though here and there some defect still reveals –
The clock strikes three but it is four,
Whose face stares back at me from the bright mirror? –
How life falls somewhat short of our ideals.

But now the forward view. Here we discover
The bedroom with the old familiar bed,
For love, or sleep, or death all sprucely spread;
It only waits the one thing or the other.

All's ready for you, see; neat as new pins
Carpets on floors, chairs upon carpets set;
The clock strikes four and it is five, and yet
The movement's onward, a new life begins.

ROBERT FRIEND

from The Teacher and the Indian

4. The Cowboy and the Indian

It was a cowboy story as he told it,
a scene out of a Western,
but with a difference,
although the setting was the expected one:
a one-street shantytown,
clapboard houses, a whorehouse and a bar
to whoop it up in.
Here came a deviation from the script:
our main characters turned out to be
a youngish cowboy and his Indian pal
only fifteen years old.

Nevertheless (returning to the script),
they whooped it up.
The cowboy leading his protégé into the bar,
taught him to drain a whiskey or a beer
at a single go, and soon they were,
as the saying has it, roaring drunk –
which the boy found much to his liking –
almost as much as what was soon to follow.
Staggering towards his horse
tethered to the hitching-post outside,
the cowboy managed to mount, making,
with the Indian pressing warmly behind him
on the one saddle, a tight fit.
Then hallooing, caterwauling, cursing,
the horse at times rearing when they suddenly drew up,
they raced up and down the soon-vacated street,

shying stones at windows, cats, stray hens,
and spraying, gloriously, bullets into the air.

This foreplay ended, the cowboy took to a road
that wound through a landscape mostly stones and hills,
but dotted occasionally with clumps of juniper.
Deciding without a word a particular clump would do,
he dismounted and lurching towards its concealing shelter,
the puzzled boy right behind him,
without forewarning stripped. Then offering
(another variation in the script)
his back to the boy, he said,
with a macho tenderness, 'Come on, kid,
give it a try.'
Overcoming his surprise and fear,
and invaded by a sudden tide of lust,
the kid did. So began
what afterwards became their usual ritual –
one that led him, about a decade later,
to invite the teacher to a bar and then himself
into his teacher's arms.

EDWIN MORGAN

Tram-Ride, 1939 (F.M.)

How cold it is to stand on the street corner
at nineteen, in the foggy Glasgow winter,
with pinched white face and hands in pockets, straining
to catch that single stocky gallus figure
who might be anyone but was one only;
prowling a few feet – not too far! – glanced at
idly by the patient Cosmo queue, growing
exposed, your watch burning, how long now, yes but,
what, half an hour, some eyes saying, Stood up eh? –
until the step has to be taken, casually,
you have to stroll off, what's won by staying?
he won't appear (he had simply forgotten,
you didn't know that then), and on the top deck
of a southbound tram you stare into the window
as it reflects a mask about to shake with
ridiculous but uncontrollable tears, a choking
you gulp back instantly, no one has heard it,
shameful – shameful – to be dominated
by such emotions as the busy tramful
of half indifferent, half curious folk would
mock at if they knew, and would they sometime,
in half a century perhaps, accept that love is
what it is, that tears are what they are, that
Jack can shiver in the numbing close-mouth
of missing dates for Jill or Jake, and suffer?

J.D. McCLATCHY

Late Night Ode

Horace IV.i

It's over, love. Look at me pushing fifty now,
    Hair like grave-grass growing in both ears,
The piles and boggy prostate, the crooked penis,
    The sour taste of each day's first lie,

And that recurrent dream of years ago pulling
    A swaying bead-chain of moonlight,
Of slipping between the cool sheets of dark
    Along a body like my own, but blameless.

What good's my cut-glass conversation now,
    Now I'm so effortlessly vulgar and sad?
You get from life what you can shake from it?
    For me, it's g and t's all day and CNN.

Try the blond boychick lawyer, entry level
    At eighty grand, who pouts about overtime,
Keeps Evian and a beeper in his locker at the gym,
    And hash in tinfoil under the office fern.

There's your hound from heaven, with buccaneer
    Curls and perfumed war-paint on his nipples.
His answering machine always has room for one more
    Slurred, embarrassed call from you-know-who.

Some nights I've laughed so hard the tears
    Won't stop. Look at me now. Why *now*?
I long ago gave up pretending to believe
    Anyone's memory will give as good as it gets

So why these stubborn tears? And why do I dream
    Almost every night of holding you again,
Or at least of diving after you, my long-gone,
    Through the bruised unbalanced waves?

RICHARD ESSENDEN

Effects

1

This is the poem I have to write.
This is the poem I have to write to you.

2

Years back, you made me a copy of your will.
Now I do whatever you require.

Your coffin slides to the furnace;
and as you go, on the tape your living fingers

stroke out the notes of
I'd like to get you

on a slow boat to China,
all by myself alone

and then I wince and almost want to giggle
as the tune shifts into

All of me, why not take all of me ...
I take the cheque,

await delivery of the TV, stereo, freezer.
And I drink the whisky left in your house

quickly, its raw warmth seeming my throat's
right, blighted inheritance.

3

The name you chose when they made you a monk.
The name of wisdom.

What happened in your childhood, and went
echoing on in mine? And later.

Back to the first cause
we can't go

but there is a sentence, commanding the child to be severed
    in two
and one part to be given to each of those claiming him.

4

Start of a spell of nearly perfect weather more than
    thirty years ago.
You walked into the quadrangle and paused,
hearing notes trickling from an open window, recognized
with a sweet shock the piano you had given up,
its tone to you as unmistakable as your mother's voice.

How many times did you tell me that?
Once you'd left, she couldn't bear to keep the keys you'd played.
A mother's love, turned to a fragrance like retribution.
She gave the piano to the old school; a year beyond her death,
you went to work there. Too neat, the way things happened
    to you.

And so it was you walked into the sun-flooded quad,
and heard that monk in his eighties trying
clumsy arpeggios in an exercise of childhood.
Months later he died in your arms
and you woke up the dormitory at one a.m. to make us pray.

What happened to those cracked, nicotined ivories?
Twenty years after, in your cramped spare bedroom
there was a brand-new baby grand you never played.
It's all like irony, but harsher.
I've given your records away.

But still I can see the fingers that had touched me
caressing some keyboard, practising some favourites:
Chopin, Brahms, Rachmaninov. You taught me to love

the ones you loved but now in my long defeat
I cherish listening to the Britten you hated
(nice touch, you watched the opera of *Death in Venice*
    with the sound off).

And in my proper life I hear clean solitary notes of Satie,
falling as if like droplets from raised oars
in a boat my unborn brother is rowing on the almost silent
    distance of a lake.

    5

Orphaned and at boarding-school,
happier away from my childless guardian's 'home',

I soon knew those corrupted kindnesses of yours,
soon depended on them.

You see, I write 'corrupted'.
Every time I try to want to write of your kindness,

I think of more to condemn.
Of course I write this only now you're dead.

6

At 13, 14, I thought I knew
I wanted to live a grown man's life.

But those Saturdays went on and on:
as the wrestling began on TV, your office-door's Yale-snib
    clicking

locked; the red light going on; then always
the slither of your palm across the backs of my bared thighs.

The heady sweetness of that green liqueur you gave me.
Embarrassments; mysteries. And arousals.

And those corrupted kindnesses of yours that I relied on.
Afterwards the sneers and jealousies of Larry Pearson,
    David Hewitt,

John and Peter Cowan, Alex Lord.
Even their fictitious names strike home.

I didn't know for years the permutations they went through
in each others' beds; or with you, in two or three locked
    rooms:

Larry and John at Larry's house one weekend;
David in shorts for you, drunk and eager, waiting hidden
    behind the desk;

Peter and Alex in the dorm after you'd been gone a week;
and, later, when Alex met you at the country-hotel, you posing
    as his uncle ...

Who was it who set off the ticking metronomes of these lives?
All of them (at 13, 14) going in with you

and hearing the click of the Yale-lock on your office-door,
all of them sent into the small back-room to change ...

To change, but to be the same forever.
That age. That look. That innocence,

but aroused, responsive. That lost thing never lost.
What of all this should be forgiven?

All of it, perhaps. None of it's ever forgotten.
I have to imagine John Cowan nearly naked close to
    midnight in your bedroom,

the rest of us sleeping in the dorm just yards away.
He knelt (you said), his elbows on your bed, like a prayer
    come true.

As he awaited you, his penis stiffening (I guess from what
    you said),
what was John thinking then? And does he wait and want
    to think of it again

now, thirty years on, even when with a woman or a wife
    perhaps?
You used to say that, in our marriages and affairs,

you'd have us always in your grip. Alex and John,
who won't read this, I wish they could tell me if it's true

desire's an unposted road, offering no other route to the island.
I wish they could speak to me the different shapes of what
    they've lived

with men or women. Where I am,
memory is sleepless, must keep on going through it all again.

The red light coming on.

The green liqueur.

The small room at the back.

The thin white cotton shorts.

Click of the lock.

7

Each night, I hear the radio's Shipping Bulletin
speak the name of where you lived.

A small, dull town.
I think of the grey sea quivering, rushing for miles

towards the pleasure-arcades, towards the white-walled
three-quarters-empty hotels.

We hardly ever tried to speak of consequences,
the distinct and random cause.

And now you've gone utterly beyond my words
as I lie listening to the radio intone its forecast,

its warning, its entrancement:
Haze. Calm. Four miles. Rising slowly.

8

When you pulled those nervous, pliant boys of 13, 14, 15
face-down across your lap,
their buttocks taut inside thin brief shorts,
what was it you were hoping for?

And the ones aged 17, 18, 19,
who needed no commanding to comply,
why did they seek with you their versions of pleasure,
    of contempt?
You'd lament they couldn't still be 13, 14, 15.

Alex, John, the others –
locked into your dream, inside an airless childhood,
they gasped at their lives,
flinching their clenched willingness against your falling hand.

9

After lights-out, the locker was opened
and I glimpsed the brunette with big breasts
lifting her soft cleavage to me, leering.

That was 1965,
the autumn I discovered masturbation,
dreaming of the fly-half of the second xv.

I shared a room with Jerzy,
the blond half-Polish boy
who wore the briefest gym-shorts in the school.

Three times in the semi-dark he revealed to me
his stash of porn-mags,
an orange drizzle from the street-lamps letting us see.

Back in our separate beds,
our hands pumped furiously under the straining sheets.
And you knew, didn't you,

just what I would be visualizing then –
the blond half-Polish boy as you had seen him,
his shorts down round his knees,

the smooth curves of his bare rump raised to your hand,
you never quite knowing how (if ever) power
transforms itself to a caress, to a version of affection.

10

What is it that sets off a life's relentless metronome?
I ask myself the obvious question
everyone will believe they have the answer to.

But things return, explained,
from before I ever knew you:
Tony, the Cunninghams, the living-room at number 5;

finding at my guardian's house a book of drawings
by Michelangelo, those thighs and muscles
the topography of an unknown homeland.

11

A decade to the day before I cremated you
(too neat, the way that everything's happened to me)
I was lying in a bed in London with a man

ten years younger than me, thirty years younger than you ...
He talked of hours when he'd imagined this, as I had:
the shock, the darkened room, the tenderness.

All I could want. All he needed from me.
But I told him nothing about this that's stayed
a kind of shame to me. In the morning

we talked like cousins or strangers.
He walked me to the Underground,
vanished for years into his marriage.

I hear that lock click shut again.

Now I'm in the back-room in the silence.

I have opened the cupboard and I'm
looking through the clothes.

I know what is expected.

I try to write the life I haven't had.

12

I listen to another music you'd have hated:
Ry Cooder's droning slide guitar, sad across the spaces
    of America.

I'd like to get away from all of this
and never come back.

I'd like to go to the high deserts of Arizona,
where nothing rusts.

That man in London shares your first name.

13

Before we scattered your ashes (paler
than I'd expected), I saw where you sat every summer
in that garden, saw the view you saw.

Your final, hidden joke,
so nakedly exposed:
the scaled-down statue of David

stood with its back to you, tense
scapula inviting a lingering caress,
the thighs so firm and smooth, his buttocks

peach-plump ... your dream come true in stone.
Always there's a question in me
whose answer does not name your name.

My fear of becoming you – the shame, the secret
exultation – the excited torment of the pages of your letters,
scattered nervously on my floor like discarded clothes.

Years back, almost emerging from a dream,
I was in a kind of garden, my fingers lingering
across a statue's smooth nude

marble buttocks – and then the figure
came to life (as Alex, as John,
as Paul or Alan) running away from me,

turning his head back laughing,
half jeering, half
luring me on.

14

Now your overcoat is
hanging in the hall; I guide
your buzzing razor round my jaw.

My bare fingers drum the keys
of the machine you've left me,
its erasing-ribbon jammed, of course.

I am typing the secret stories of my life.
They end, don't they, they finally
exhaust every trivial, thrilling word.

15

This is not the poem I have to write.
This is not the poem I have to write to you.

As we drove to burn you,
I saw through the car's window
a class of boys, fifteen perhaps,
playing touch-rugby on a narrow field.

At home again, I sit
with more of your whisky in my hand,
forging my freedom,
waiting for your effects.

GREGORY WOODS

Andy

Here and again
here, I keep on
coming back to
this place, as though
I had been born

in its shadows
or wanted to
relive some dead
passion of my
youth in its heat.

It is the kind
of fastness I
could move to for
good, if not for
the snag that an

adolescent's
perineum
offers nothing
more steady than
no fixed abode.

STEVE CRANFIELD

Gym Class of '67 (Summer of Love)

How it was. Pat Stack, lanky, loth to wear
A top, his tight shorts always lingering
Over slim hips. Pat Shallow, coal-black hair
In curls, pellucid nipples blistering
His marble pecs. Geoff Tompkins, tanned broad chest,
The first to flaunt an adult's cock and bush.
Paul Grubiak, in many ways the thickest,
Fore and aft. Steve Cranfield, needing a push
To lose his vest. Kev Hartnett, smart Y-fronts,
Easing his balls into their soft white pouch.
Dick Green, gym master, sunning himself once
On pitch (not showering, alas!). To touch
This side of sweaty sleep proving unable ...
Writing, one hand still gropes beneath the table.

TIM NEAVE

Poem: L.M.C.

It was the smallest moment I've known
in some ways. Hardly the start
of what should change me.
                                But it's
with me always, like a mist
burned off from the beach –
the familiar details; the knowledge it was there.

There is not a picture in this.
Anyone who painted that street
would miss the closeness almost completely
of its ordinary grandeur, and
in trying to write about it like this
I acknowledge how far I am
from being a part of what I want.

Listen to the meaninglessness of this:
I want an ordinary boy,
a fishworker in jeans or overalls,
boots and the stench of fish,
splashed with the skin and guts of fish;
I want to drink with him
in a fisherman's pub on Freeman Street
and lose myself to the same stupor
he spoke through when we stopped to talk
outside the Kent Arms a week back.
If there's a poetry in this
is it to do with the beauty of being there,
the realistic people stunned by alcohol
into serenity and community, or is it

an educated outsider's tragic desire
knocked against the concrete of a hard world?

I want a particular boy
in slack jeans and a dirty shirt,
pulling that smile from his caution
that lights up everything, like a flare;
a flare that soars then collapses
till its brightness penetrates the water's cold
and the same blackness hasn't gone
although there's someone searching there
and the rescuer and rescued are as one
in that the tragedy or heroism of it all
is not decided, in that we're both at sea
hoping to find another human being
who will reclaim meaning from the shocked void.

These words I play with here,
it's just me laughing at myself,
enjoying the pretence of largeness
in my particular despair. I mock.

I have touched him and smelled him.
The basic sensations of my love for him
are animal, which persuades me
of their complete worth. How different they are
from the togetherness of friendship
or the couples shopping on this street.
How strange that the image which comes
if I permit myself an open mind
is the spurt of my semen against his neck
that's newly shaved and raw
like it was the first time I wanted to touch him
that November morning in a classroom
when he showed up for the first time in weeks
and laughed like he was somehow different
from the blond-haired boy I had seen before,

like now he had acquired new needs
that he needed a different space for
from the inhumane restrictions of school.
I don't know what he wanted from that day,
nor those later unscheduled meetings we had
to talk through his prospects for exams;
but I hope I played my part for him,
even if that's to be the end of it.
It enlarges my heart to know I've helped,
and in some awful sense it's enough
if he ever thinks of me and smiles.

A huge space opens, and these things aren't real
so much as abstractions around a theme,
an essay on the poverty of human love
between two people of the same sex
that lacks the awesomeness that made me write it.
A white-caught gull against the wind
that's more a symbol than a bird.
And that isn't what I meant.

PETER WYLES

Beauty

Make him into a stained glass window,
a shrine lit by a thousand candles,
an icon as big as a wall.
He's used to worship.

We could have the relics here,
his favourite brand of hair conditioner,
the button-fly Levis he might have worn,
the sole remaining photograph.

We've nothing he touched, but us,
nothing he owned as memento.
He was the briefest of love's Messiahs,
who returned through cloud to Warrington.

Nothing less than bowing down
will do. We must contemplate
the perfection of his outward form,
the virile beauty of his cock,
the limp flesh of his excuses.

IESTYN EDWARDS

Of Course I Do

I walked to the end of that street,
Saw the overshot bridge
Whose grey walls are warmed
By tight graffiti;

Heard, but didn't see,
Cars stalking past
And flutes shrilling
From a whitewashed Suffolk church:
Why did you show this to me?

You know that I scorn,
In argument and passion,
The comfort of compromise;
You darkly cringe to shoulder the burden –
Burial of together.

But, grinning mercurially, louche canines glowing,
You ask me what else can I show?

A velvet voice, gondola black,
Dredging our tear-warmed sea,
Echoes from a backdrop
Of moon tie-dyed twilight,
To strengthen my tears
And coax my vessel on:
Heart's horizon of our passion bound.

Ahead, you reach up and shape for me
A weather shield
From a corner of heaven.
Look back into the middle-distance;
Tell me what you see.

I see an olive grove,
A stumbling kid goat
And silent late afternoon.

DINYAR GODREJ

Anyone could succumb ...

Anyone could succumb to those eyes
and, being drawn, find
disconcerting silence.

Search instead the domestic terrain
for faultlines,
mnemonic chinks.

There are no photographs
and everything comes from far off,
settled in dust.

So, again, imagine
urgent love beside the steady clock
a floor above the heaped sink:

as though our impulse was the sea,
its rushing spume
lust not fury.

This rolling game of getting on top,
hot exploration,
sticky end.

Yet memory stays sealed, adrift.
We exhale, everything subsides,
so rest.

Limbs interlaced in the warm containing bath,
eyes lock.
It brims but does not spill.

IV AS IT IS

'As it is, plenty ... ' as Auden said. The poems gathered here tell of gay love as it is: seldom uncomplicated, seldom uninteresting. Some affairs end in tears, others in laughter. Sometimes a moment is etched into a single exact emblem, as in Robert Friend's 'Shirts' or Francis King's 'The Bank-Notes'; elsewhere, the external world intervenes with odd or ironic messages – the mathematician's 'true passion' chalked on a blackboard in Thom Gunn's 'The Problem', the sign warning 'Beware of Trains' in Adam Johnson's 'Unscheduled Stop'.

The tones range from heartfelt directness – Shakespeare's 'Sonnet 29', Edwin Morgan's 'Dear man, my love goes out in waves ... ' – to no less moving obliquity: Paul Wilkins writes, meaningfully, of an inability to say just what he means, while Steve Cranfield contributes a love poem about not writing a love poem.

MICHELANGELO

Translated by J.A. Symonds

To Tommaso de' Cavalieri

With your fair eyes a charming light I see,
For which my own blind eyes would peer in vain;
Stayed by your feet the burden I sustain
Which my lame feet find all too strong for me;

Wingless upon your pinions forth I fly;
Heavenward your spirit stirreth me to strain;
E'en as you will I blush and blanch again,
Freeze in the sun, burn 'neath a frosty sky.

Your will includes and is the lord of mine;
Life to my thoughts within your heart is given;
My words begin to breathe upon your breath:

Like to the moon am I, that cannot shine
Alone; for lo! our eyes see nought in heaven
Save what the living sun illumineth.

*

Why should I seek to ease intense desire
With still more tears and windy words of grief,
When heaven, or late or soon, sends no relief
To souls whom love hath robed around with fire?

Why need my aching heart to death aspire,
When all must die? Nay, death beyond belief
Unto these eyes would be both sweet and brief,
Since in my sum of woes all joys expire!

Therefore, because I cannot shun the blow
I rather seek, say who must rule my breast,
Gliding between her gladness and her woe?

If only chains and bands can make me blest,
No marvel if alone and bare I go
An armèd Knight's captive and slave confessed.

MICHAEL DRAYTON

from Idea

To nothing fitter can I thee compare
Than to the son of some rich pennyfather,
Who, having now brought on his end with care,
Leaves to his son all he had heaped together;
This new rich novice, lavish of his chest,
To one man gives, doth on another spend,
Then here he riots, yet among the rest
Haps to lend some to one true honest friend.
Thy gifts thou in obscurity doth waste,
False friends thy kindness, born but to deceive thee,
Thy love that is on the unworthy placed,
Time hath thy beauty, which with age will leave thee;
    Only that little which to me was lent
    I give thee back, when all the rest is spent.

WILLIAM SHAKESPEARE

Sonnet 29

When in disgrace with Fortune and men's eyes,
I all alone beweep my outcast state,
And trouble deaf heaven with my bootless cries,
And look upon myself and curse my fate,
Wishing me like to one more rich in hope,
Featured like him, like him with friends possessed,
Desiring this man's art, and that man's scope,
With what I most enjoy contented least;
Yet in these thoughts myself almost despising,
Haply I think on thee, and then my state,
Like to the lark at break of day arising
From sullen earth, sings hymns at heaven's gate;
    For thy sweet love rememb'red such wealth brings,
    That then I scorn to change my state with kings.

WILLIAM SHAKESPEARE

Sonnet 87

Farewell, thou art too dear for my possessing,
And like enough thou know'st thy estimate:
The charter of thy worth gives thee releasing;
My bonds in thee are all determinate.
For how do I hold thee but by thy granting,
And for that riches where is my deserving?
The cause of this fair gift in me is wanting,
And so my patent back again is swerving.
Thyself thou gav'st, thy own worth then not knowing,
Or me, to whom thou gav'st it, else mistaking;
So thy great gift, upon misprision growing,
Comes home again, on better judgement making.
   Thus have I had thee as a dream doth flatter,
   In sleep a king, but waking no such matter.

WILLIAM SHAKESPEARE

from Troilus and Cressida

Patroclus	To this effect, Achilles, have I mov'd you.
	A woman impudent and manish grown
	Is not more loath'd than an effeminate man
	In time of action. I stand condemn'd for this:
	They think my little stomach to the war
	And your great love to me restrains you thus.
	Sweet, rouse yourself; and the weak wanton Cupid
	Shall from your neck unloose his amorous fold,
	And, like a dew-drop from the lion's mane,
	Be shook to air.
Achilles	Shall Ajax fight with Hector?
Patroclus	Ay, and perhaps receive much honour by him.
Achilles	I see my reputation is at stake;
	My fame is shrewdly gor'd.
Patroclus	O then beware;
	Those wounds heal ill that men do give themselves.
	Omission to do what is necessary
	Seals a commission to a blank of danger;
	And danger, like an ague, subtly taints
	Even then when we sit idly in the sun.
Achilles	Go call Thersites hither, sweet Patroclus.
	I'll send the fool to Ajax, and desire him
	T'invite the Trojan lords after the combat
	To see us here unarm'd. I have a woman's longing,
	An appetite that I am sick withal,
	To see great Hector in his weeds of peace,
	To talk with him, and to behold his visage
	Even to my full of view.

[III: III: 216–42]

RICHARD BARNFIELD

To His Friend Master R.L.,
in Praise of Music and Poetry

If music and sweet poetry agree,
As they must needs, the sister and the brother,
Then must the love be great 'twixt thee and me,
Because thou lov'st the one, and I the other.
Dowland to thee is dear, whose heavenly touch
Upon the lute doth ravish human sense;
Spenser, to me, whose deep conceit is such
As, passing all conceit, needs no defence.
Thou lov'st to hear the sweet melodious sound
That Phoebus' lute, the queen of music, makes;
And I in deep delight am chiefly drowned
Whenas himself to singing he betakes:
    One god is god of both, as poets feign;
    One knight loves both, and both in thee remain.

WALT WHITMAN

from Calamus

Hours continuing long, sore and heavy-hearted,
Hours of the dusk, when I withdraw to a lonesome and
    unfrequented spot, seating myself, leaning my face
    in my hands;
Hours sleepless, deep in the night, when I go forth, speeding
    swiftly the country roads, or through the city streets,
    or pacing miles and miles, stifling plaintive cries;
Hours discouraged, distracted – for the one I cannot content
    myself without, soon I saw him content himself without me;
Hours when I am forgotten, (O weeks and months are passing,
    but I believe I am never to forget!)
Sullen and suffering hours! (I am ashamed – but it is useless –
    I am what I am;)
Hours of my torment – I wonder if other men ever have
    the like, out of the like feelings?
Is there even one other like me – distracted – his friend,
    his lover, lost to him?
Is he too as I am now? Does he still rise in the morning,
    dejected, thinking who is lost to him? and at night,
    awaking, think who is lost?
Does he too harbour his friendship silent and endless?
    harbour his anguish and passion?
Does some stray reminder, or casual mention of a name,
    bring the fit back upon him, taciturn and deprest?
Doe he see himself reflected in me? In these hours,
    does he see the face of his hours reflected?

WILFRED OWEN

To Eros

In that I loved you, Love, I worshipped you.
In that I worshipped well, I sacrificed.
All of most worth I bound and burnt and slew:
Old peaceful lives; frail flowers; firm friends; and Christ.

I slew all falser loves; I slew all true,
That I might nothing love but your truth, Boy.
Fair fame I cast away as bridegrooms do
Their wedding garments in their haste of joy.

But when I fell upon your sandalled feet,
You laughed; you loosed away my lips; you rose.
I heard the singing of your wings' retreat;
Far-flown, I watched you flush the Olympian snows,
Beyond my hoping. Starkly I returned
To stare upon the ash of all I burned.

ROBERT FRIEND

Shirts

Rereading Cavafy I suddenly remembered
my own Ionian Sea, and a steamer
plying between the islands.
And I remembered, amidst the passengers
crowding the deck of the steamer,
a handsome young Greek
wearing a shirt I very much admired,
and he in turn admiring mine.

We took off our shirts then and there
and exchanged them.

I wore his shirt next to my skin
for many years.
But it was never the same on my body
as on his, and he was not there
to take it off.

EDWIN MORGAN

'Dear man, my love goes out in waves ... '

Dear man, my love goes out in waves
and breaks. Whatever is, craves.
Terrible the cage
to see all life from, brilliantly about,
crowds, pavements, cars, or hear the common shout
of goals in a near park.
But now the black bars arc
blue in my breath – split – part –
I'm out – it's art,
it's love, it's rage –

Standing in rage in decent air
will never clear the place of care.
Simply to be
should be enough, in the same city, and let
absurd despair tramp and roar off-set.
Be satisfied with it,
the gravel and the grit
the struggling eye can't lift,
the veils that drift,
the weird to dree.

Press close to me at midnight as
you say goodbye; that's what it has
to offer, life
I mean. Into the frost with you; into
the bed with me; and get the light out too.
Better to shake unseen
and let real darkness screen
the shadows of the heart,
the vacant part-
ner, husband, wife.

FRANCIS KING

The Bank-Notes

Really there is little enough I shall care now to remember
   And perhaps this only, the thirst, the dust and the terror
      of being alone,
Darkness that evening of August – or might it have been
      September?
   And flesh that burned on flesh, and the hard, cold touch
      of stone.

Really there is little enough to remember. And time confuses
   Such nights, reality with dream and loss with lack,
So perhaps that night does not exist to which my mind
      now chooses,
   Obstinately chooses now to twist and still twist back.

Yet surely it must exist: for how clearly I remember
   The sound of tearing bank-notes as we struggled beneath
      the trees
That far-off evening of August – or was it perhaps September? –
   And the sweat upon that face and the blood upon my knees.

It had all seemed long forgotten; it is only now as I stand
   Waiting for the men to come to carry my trunks away
That I feel those lips on my lips, that hand within my hand,
   And again the two taut bodies lunge outwards and clutch
      and sway.

THOM GUNN

The Problem

Close to the top
Of an encrusted dark
Converted brownstone West of Central Park
(For this was 1961),
In his room that
               a narrow hutch
Was sliced from some once-cavernous flat,
Where now a window took a whole wall up
And tints were bleached-out by the sun
Of many a summer day,
We lay
       upon his hard thin bed.

He seemed all body, such
As normally you couldn't touch,
Reckless and rough,
One of Boss Cupid's red-
                    haired errand boys
Who couldn't get there fast enough.
Almost like fighting ...
We forgot about the noise,
But feeling turned so self-delighting
That hurry soon gave way
To give-and-take,
Till each contested, for the other's sake,
To end up not in winning and defeat
But in a draw.

Meanwhile beyond the aureate hair
I saw
A scrap of blackboard with its groove for chalk,
Nailed to a strip of lath
That had half-broken through,
The problem drafted there
                              still incomplete.
After I found out in the talk
Companion to a cigarette,
That he, turning the problem over yet
In his disorderly and ordered head,
Attended graduate school to teach
And study math,
                    his true
Passion cyphered in chalk beyond my reach.

ROGER FINCH

A Publicity Photograph

Butch. You are no poet, you are not
sweet Thomas Chatterton blacking out
limply at eighteen across his bed
in the chiaroscuro of his attic,
you are Butch, the neighbourhood bully, whose threat

'I'll beat you to a pulp' simply because
I was the neighbourhood sissy almost
came true, his thumbnail inside my cheek,
his teeth clamped on my earlobe so hard
it must have been passion. You, at least,

have an easy smile and easy eyes.
But look, you have the same wire-haired terrier hair,
the same brutal brows, the same bull neck.
And why are you wearing that black leather
jacket and that black T-shirt that from where

I am standing reads '...lgar...' or '...dgar...'
in white? You are threatening me. I touch
my ear, believing your strong white teeth
made the scar there, I touch other parts
of my body, believing your hands can reach

me from where you are sitting in that white
kitchen chair, intimately. Your words
are full of subjected women who moan
as they twist around you but I believe
I could teach your body to lie still on the floorboards

or the moss-softened rocks as I lower
myself in the attitude of a cross
upon you, the fluttering white wings
of my chest beating against your chest.
I want that first real surreptitious kiss.

J.D. McCLATCHY

After Ovid

Apollo and Hyacinthus

Guilt's dirty hands, memory's kitchen sink ...
    It's bad faith makes immortal love.
        Take a closer look at Hyacinth.

Dark bud-tight curls and poppy-seed stubble,
    The skin over his cheekbones pale as poison
        Slowly dripped from eye to eye,

And a crotch that whispers its single secret
    Even from behind the waiter's apron.
        He's pouting now, staring at the traffic.

Every year there's a new one at the bar
    Sprung from whatever nowhere – the country,
        The islands, the middle west ...

The old man at the far corner table, decades ago
    Called by his critics 'the sun god
        Of our poetry', sits stirring

A third coffee and an opening line,
    Something like *So often you renew
        Yourself* or *You and I resemble*

~~Nothing else~~ *Every other pair of lovers.*
    The grease stain on his left sleeve
        Winks as the lights come on.

He signals the boy and means to ask
   Under cover of settling the check
      If, with the usual understanding

And for the same pleasures, he'd return again
   Tonight, after work, there was something
      He'd wanted to show the boy, a picture

Of two sailors that if held upside down ...
   It's then he notices the gold cufflinks
      The boy is wearing, the pair the poet's

Friends had given him when his first book –
   That moist sheaf of stifled longings –
      Appeared in Alexandria.

To have stolen from one who would give
   Anything: what better pretext
      To put the end to 'an arrangement'?

The old man falls silent, gets up from his seat,
   Leaves a few coins on the table
      And walks out through his confusions,

Homeward through the sidestreets, across the square,
   Up the fifty-two stone steps, up the years
      And back to his study, its iron cot.

The heaving had stopped. The last sad strokes
   Of the town clock had rung: Anger was one,
      Humiliation the other.

He sat there until dawn and wrote out the poem
   That has come to be in all the anthologies,
      The one you know, beginning

You are my sorrow and my fault. The one that goes
    In all my songs, in my mind, in my mouth,
      The sighing still sounds of you.

The one that ends with the boy – the common,
    Adored, two-timing hustler – turned
      Into a flower, *the soft-fleshed lily*

But of a bruised purple that grief will come
    To scar with its initials AI, AI.
      O, the ache insists.

MICHAEL SCHMIDT

'His father was a baker ... '
for A.G.G.

His father was a baker, he the youngest son.
I understand they beat him, and they loved him.

His father was a baker in Oaxaca:
I understand his bakery was the best

And his three sons and all his daughters helped
As children with the baking and the pigs.

I can imagine chickens in their patio,
At Christmastime a wattled turkey-cock, a dog

Weathered like a wash-board, yellow-eyed,
That no one stroked, but ate the scraps of bread

And yapped to earn his keep. I understand
The family prospered though the father drank

And now the second brother drinks, often
To excess. I understand as well that love

Came early, bladed, and then went away
And came again in other forms, some foreign,

And took him by the heart away from home.
His father was a baker in Oaxaca

And here I smell the loaves that rose in ovens
Throughout a childhood not yet quite complete

And smell the fragrance of his jet-black hair,
Taste his sweet dialect that is mine too,

Until I understand I am to be a baker,
Up before dawn wth trays and trays of dough

To feed him this day, next day and for ever –
Or for a time – the honey-coloured loaves.

NEIL POWELL

The Difference

We watch the gathering sea through sepia dusk
Across a beach of fish-heads, glass beads, relics
Dumped by a careless deity called chance.
Ferry and trawler exchange a passing glance.

Dark comes fast: lighthouse and streetlamp pierce it.
You sit at the window, silent as I write.
We are no longer locked in self-defence.
Being with you has made all the difference.

PAUL WILKINS

Glasnost'

The month Ivan's and Misha's tank whined
juddering into Wenceslas Square,
I passed O-level Russian.

'Fascinating,' grins Alastair,
who is listening to these lines.

August 1968: 'Socialism's human face' was
Dubcek's, a poster on a Clapham bedroom wall, his thin mouth
smiling under tired, vulture eyes. In Croydon we heard
Prague Radio crackling, deciphered the chalked tank-turrets'
'Volodya, go home! Your Anna is with Fyodor!'

I still have some of the Russian words.
Kak vas zavoot? I can ask someone.
'What do they call you?' 'What is your name?'
Chai s'limonom, parzhalsta. I can order a cup of lemon tea.
I know that *Glasnost'* must be a noun.

And I remember Lenin's question: What is to be done?
The man who taught us how to ask *Shto delat'?* was
'obviously queer'. That August
he tried to persuade me I should take the subject further.
I went for Economics, collaborated in the rumours.

Throughout that year, Chris had sat two desks ahead of me.
First in our class to wear flared trousers,
he knew irregular Greek verbs and the Russian for
'I understand the lesson for today.'
I didn't and don't.

I know that at the end of *Glasnost'* is a sound
my language can't write down.
The 'soft sign', they call it. It's a little
'tch' of tenderness, a gentle chafing of the teeth and tongue.
No, that's not it.

'But you can say *it, can't you? And who was Chris?' Alastair
pours us beers. 'And Lenin – for Christ's sake, Lenin!'*

Decades on, two pairs of flares hang
embarrassed in my wardrobe. I open the window
on an August night in London, and the raining random noise
spits in and on:

traffic; the pulse of music from the Seventh Day Adventist Hall;
a dog two streets away,
barking with furious thirst or boredom,
chafing at the chain of speech he does not have.

In the paper Boris Zhikov, aged 16,
clutches his signed LP above a headline:
Children of Perestroika Meet the Pet Shop Boys.

I close and lock the window.
I watch my video of Horovitz
playing at last again in Moscow after sixty years.
Rachmaninov, Scriabin, Schumann's *Kinderszenen.*
During the 'Träumerei' encore, a tear slides down an old man's
        cheek.

*'The trouble with your poems is,' says Alastair,
'you don't say enough about your feelings.'*

I rehearse the phrases that have stayed:
Kak menya zavoot? and *Shto delat'?*
What do they call me? What is to be done?
A sound of tenderness, is it?
The teeth against the tongue.

'But you can say it, can't you?' Alastair repeats.
He finishes his beer and grins again.
'And by the way, that isn't how you spell my name.'

The dictionary I found this summer translates
Glasnost' as, not 'openness', but 'publicity'.

At its end is something I can't yet write down.

GREGORY WOODS

Reconciliation

If there were dancers, they were not dancing. If there was
    a tree,
It had not emerged from the rock. Potential was enough.
Fish, if there were fish, confined themselves discreetly
    to the dark
Angles in the shadow of the overhang, if the moon was out
For casting shadows. (Say, for the sake of the moment, it was.)

In the presence of the dust, we celebrated our return
To sanity. It was the dust we tasted on each other's skin –
You could say we made mud of it. Adapting our accustomed
Falsehoods to the requirement of the time, we reduced
    each other's
Serious intensity to laughter, an excuse for tears.

If there was a clock, hidden under blankets in a basket
Or thieved by brigands in the night, it would not for want
    of winding
Stop. We were reconciled to that. I slept in your armpit,
    dreaming,
If there were dreams, of you: *you* in the mountains,
    you on horseback,
You at the cash-and-carry. There was a sentence which recurred

In every episode. I knew it was the same but couldn't
Have repeated any single word of it on waking up.
Who said it, you or I or the kid at the check-out, was open
To interpretation. I think I spoke it when you woke me
But your kisses tightened on me like a buckled rubber gag.

STEVE CRANFIELD

The Testament
for Bryan

> Ming not your lufe with fals deceptioun.
> Beir in your mynd this short conclusioun
> Of fair Cresseid – as I have said befoir;
> Sen scho is deid, I speik of hir no moir.
>   Henryson, *The Testament of Cresseid*

'You must write me a poem some day ...
Provided it's something you really mean
        I can be patient,' I heard you say
Once, blowing smoke-rings from the bed
As I unbalanced, one leg into my jeans.
Only when I'd opened, fully dressed,
Your 'special gift' – a biro and blank pad –
Did I wake up to a serious request.

What's it to me, though, anonymised *Lines to X*?
Or the authorised task of staining paper sheets
        As an alternative to sex?
Wasn't it the bane of writers in the past,
Having to be in sync with the dictates
Of pea-brained nobles, God or The Mistress?
Well-heeled academics feel 'coerced'
By equivalent calls from the Murdoch press.

Maybe I read too much into your present,
Detecting hints of 'All this was commission
        But were you equal to it?' I wasn't.
Commissions, poems, end. Lust, likewise, vanishes.

Not that I gave much weight to your opposition
The day I declined to end things over-the-top:
An unfussed character, shorn of flourishes.
I know the value of the one full stop.

And yet, I find myself writing the thing
You asked for but would feel puzzled to receive
        (You shan't), the whole time wondering
What it is prompts me to arrange words unsaid,
Unsayable, to you in person, deceives
Me into thinking I can beyond where
Henryson left his polished-off Cresseid:
'Sen scho is deid, I speik of hir no moir.'

His stern anti-metaphysical tact
(Rare in a medieval) pulls me up short
        With its callous, matter-of-fact
Reminder that deception has its limits.
Obeying your one proviso never taught
Me to doubt that meant poems haunt the lonely
Or that, for all would-be securities, it's
The idiot who writes to commissions only.

PETER DANIELS

Assessment

David Jones lacks motivation.
He has failed to achieve his targets
for three months. His timekeeping is poor.
His attitude leaves much to be desired.

David's appearance is hard to fault
and I must say he does attract
attention, but somehow it's always
in the wrong way. It's fine to look good
but sales must always be our number one priority.

David is brilliant but erratic. The clients
find him unsettling. His smile
can undermine office morale for days
and days. Last week I pulled him up
for an untidy desk, and his face
lit the room most embarrassingly.

His carefree songs at the computer
can move certain colleagues to tears, which
is bad for productivity.
This kind of thing gets personal,
and management's no picnic at the best of times.
It can't go on.

For the good of our company I shall have to
let him go. I can't hold on to an employee like David.

DAVID KINLOCH

Bed
for Eric

The moment the light goes out,
He sleeps: a gift from the dark.
There is the small chime
Of the moon on the wall,
The deep freeze digesting
In the kitchen. He floats
From head to toe on the buzz
Of his snore, dreaming the calm
Glide of a Jaspar ski-lift,
The summer elk that trotted
Out of forest beneath our
Dangling feet. His arm
Crooks the violin of my head.
I elbow him away intent on
Sleep but suddenly unpegged
By a gust of dreams we roll
Together in the hot hole
Of his mum's old bed,
Dribbling on the pillows.
Waking, he has me in an
Arm-lock, our legs a single
Rope of flesh, my ear-lobe
Tickled by his breath. I reach
Behind me and shove my hand
Between his thighs. He stretches,
Opening briefly like a centre-
Fold, a light smile of welcome

On his lips. But more than this
Is the scrape of the two-o'clock
Beetle, the nip of a dust-mite,
My scratch: my love disturbed
By me, awake but patient
In the dark.

STEVE ANTHONY

A Good Fit

A score of hopefuls, then we fitted:
same height, same build, a pairing so neat
I'd wear your jeans to hug me tight
and we'd stroll touch-close along the street

counting the smiles. We made love all the time –
morning and night, the long light
afternoons, in bed, or the rougher climb
of the stairs, the sink, everywhere was right.

The best time, on the living room rug,
I followed your skin like the coast on a map,
you spread your legs and I backed in, snug,
your arms closing round me, moored in your lap.

Then we locked together to pull and collide,
two men matched in sweat and feeling,
till we lay back, done in, side by side,
laughing up to the stucco ceiling.

For days we didn't bother with clothes.
Evenings, cuddled out the colder weather;
unless we'd filled them with wine and friends
to show how good we were together ...

But in dancing crowds we came apart,
slipped off into the world again;
I was left out on the midnight street
like a fashionable shoe in the rain.

JOEL LANE

Sandman

You know what the day feels like
after a sleepless night. A coach station
in late spring, rainy with voices,
dissent beaten down by unconcern;
or travelling back from the coast
with sand grains lodged in the folds
of your clothes. The light is cramped.
You never clear the oxygen debt.

Meanwhile, the latent dreams will
have their say in daylight:
a furious proliferation of images,
layer on layer of thin action, compressed;
pages the censor and the pornographer
sat up together to make. Some people
behave as though they never slept;
their memories are only skin deep.

Dreams is too comfortable a word
for the thoughts of mine you hold
in restless hands, a cat's cradle
that you can't tighten or unpick.
Does it make you feel strong
to play the sandman with me
like this, to hurt and comfort?
It sounds bitter now, to say:

when I slept with you, the best thing,
and sometimes the only thing, was the sleep.

PETER WYLES

Bird Flight

Frost on the bare ribs of ploughed earth,
the low V of ducks over mist and water,
the turn of a high bird against the sky,
first one way, a call, and then the other.

Last night on my hands and in my mouth,
two fists of wool, the smell of smoke,
and in a pocket his unearned lighter.

What I look for is wherever I am,
what has to be said cannot be said,
staring to the core of this frozen flower.
First one way, a call, and then the other.

ADAM JOHNSON

Unscheduled Stop

I sit in the *Charles Hallé*
At windy Manningtree,
While gulls enact their ballet
Above the estuary.

'We seem to have some problem ... '
A faltering voice explains.
I spy, along the platform,
A sign: 'Beware of trains'

And picture you, impatient,
In the car park at the back
Of a gaudy toy-town station,
Or craning down the track,

As the afternoon rehearses
An evensong of birds –
Our time in the hands of others,
And too brief for words.

LAWRENCE SCHIMEL

Palimpsest

Can you feel, as your fingers dance across
my back, the marks of all the men
who've touched me before you –
their fingers clawing stripes across my flesh
as we made love, or kneading deep,
as you do, massaging away tension, stress?
I feel that even their lightest caresses
have scarred me permanently, branding me
as surely as the kiss of leather straps and whips.

Is it some sleight-of-hand trick you do
that makes my body feel fresh and pure?
What is this legerdemain that, although your hands
have travelled this stretch of flesh so many
times before, this path stretching from shoulder
down along the spine to the ass, that makes it seem
new each time, that this is unexplored territory?

Surely your fingers must feel the imprints
of all those earlier passions, as they now awaken
such strong feelings in me again. I open my
mouth to tell you, as I lie before you, naked and
pliable, but your fingers press deep
into muscle – and I lose all will.

V BORDERLINES

Several of this group are ungendered love poems which have been gratefully adopted by gay men, beginning with a favourite of my own (Fulke Greville's 'Absence, the noble truce ... ') and including a couple suggested by other contributors to this book. Perhaps the most controversial of these is the extract from *Peter Grimes*, which hardly looks like a love poem; but it seems beyond doubt that Crabbe's twentieth-century admirers E.M. Forster and, thanks to him, Benjamin Britten, were drawn by the poem's homosexual sub-text and that the relationship between Grimes and his apprentices is one of thwarted love.

I've also included two eighteenth-century extracts – by Pope and Churchill – which are *about* gay love: the period is otherwise under-represented, and it may be salutary to have some indication of how others see (or rather *saw*) us.

FULKE GREVILLE

from Caelica

Absence, the noble truce
Of Cupid's war:
Where though desires want use,
They honoured are.
Thou art the just protection
Of prodigal affection,
Have thou the praise;
When bankrupt Cupid braveth,
Thy mines his credit saveth,
With sweet delays.

Of wounds which presence makes
With beauty's shot,
Absence the anguish slakes,
But healeth not:
Absence records the stories,
Wherein desire glories,
Although she burn;
She cherisheth the spirits
Where constancy inherits
And passions mourn.

Absence, like dainty clouds,
On glorious bright,
Nature's weak senses shrouds
From harming light.
Absence maintains the treasure
Of pleasure unto pleasure,
Sparing with praise;
Absence doth nurse the fire,
Which starves and feeds desire
With sweet delays.

Presence to every part
Of beauty ties,
Where wonder rules the heart
There pleasure dies:
Pleasure plagues mind and senses
With modesty's defences,
Absence is free:
Thoughts do in absence venter
On Cupid's shadowed centre,
They wink and see.

But thoughts be not so brave,
With absent joy;
For you with that you have
Yourself destroy:
The absence which you glory,
Is that which makes you sorry,
And burn in vain:
For thought is not the weapon,
Wherewith thought's ease men cheapen,
Absence is pain.

MICHAEL DRAYTON

'Since there's no help ... '

Since there's no help, come, let us kiss and part –
Nay, I have done: you get no more of me;
And I am glad, yea, glad with all my heart
That thus so cleanly I myself can free.
Shake hands forever, cancel all our vows,
And when we meet at any time again,
Be it not seen in either of our brows
That we one jot of former love retain.
Now at the last gasp of love's latest breath,
When, his pulse failing, Passion speechless lies,
When Faith is kneeling by his bed of death,
And Innocence is closing up his eyes –
    Now, if thou would'st, when all have given him over,
    From death to life thou might'st him yet recover.

ANDREW MARVELL

The Definition of Love

I

My love is of a birth as rare
As 'tis for object strange and high:
It was begotten by Despair
Upon Impossibility.

II

Magnanimous Despair alone
Could show me so divine a thing,
Where feeble Hope could ne'er have flown
But vainly flapped its tinsel wing.

III

And yet I quickly might arrive
Where my extended soul is fixed,
But Fate does iron wedges drive,
And always crowds itself betwixt.

IV

For Fate with jealous eye does see
Two perfect loves, nor lets them close:
Their union would her ruin be,
And her tyrannic power depose.

V

And therefore her decrees of steel
Us as the distant Poles have placed,
(Though Love's whole world on us doth wheel)
Not by themselves to be embraced,

VI

Unless the giddy heaven fall,
And earth some new convulsion tear;
And, us to join, the world should all
Be cramped into a planisphere.

VII

As lines (so loves) oblique may well
Themselves in every angle greet:
But ours so truly parallel,
Though infinite, can never meet.

VIII

Therefore the love which us doth bind,
But Fate so enviously debars,
Is the conjunction of the mind,
And opposition of the stars.

JOHN DRYDEN

from The Maiden Queen

I feed a flame which so torments me
That it both pains my heart and yet contents me:
'Tis such a pleasing smart and I so love it,
That I had rather die, then once remove it.

Yet he for whom I grieve shall never know it,
My tongue does not betray, nor my eyes show it:
Not a sigh not a tear my pain discloses,
But they fall silently like dew on roses.

Thus to prevent my love from being cruel,
My heart's the sacrifice as 'tis the fuel:
And while I suffer thus to give him quiet,
My faith rewards my love, though he deny it.

On his eyes will I gaze, and there delight me;
Where I conceal my love, no frown can fright me:
To be more happy I dare not aspire;
Nor can I fall more low, mounting no higher.

ALEXANDER POPE

from An Epistle from Mr Pope, to Dr Arbuthnot

Let Sporus tremble – 'What? that Thing of silk,
Sporus, that mere white Curd of Ass's milk?
Satire or Sense alas! can Sporus feel?
Who breaks a Butterfly upon a Wheel?
Yet let me flap this Bug with gilded wings,
This painted Child of Dirt that stinks and stings;
Whose Buzz the Witty and the Fair annoys,
Yet Wit ne'er tastes, and Beauty ne'er enjoys,
So well-bred Spaniels civilly delight
In mumbling of the Game they dare not bite.
Eternal Smiles his Emptiness betray,
As shallow streams run dimpling all the way.
Whether in florid Impotence he speaks,
And, as the Prompter breathes, the Puppet squeaks;
Or at the Ear of Eve, familiar Toad,
Half Froth, half Venom, spits himself abroad,
In Puns, or Politics, or Tales, or Lies,
Or Spite, or Smut, or Rhymes, or Blasphemies.
His Wit all see-saw between *that* and *this*,
Now high, now low, now Master up, now Miss,
And he himself one vile Antithesis.
Amphibious Thing! that acting either Part,
The trifling Head, or the corrupted Heart!
Fop at the Toilet, Flatt'rer at the Board,
Now trips a Lady, and now struts a Lord.
Eve's Tempter thus the Rabbins have expressed,
A Cherub's face, a Reptile all the rest;
Beauty that shocks you, Parts that none will trust,
Wit that can creep, and Pride that licks the dust.

[305–33]

CHRISTOPHER SMART

Hymn 13: St Philip and St James

Now the winds are all composure,
    But the breath upon the bloom,
Blowing sweet o'er each inclosure,
    Grateful off'rings of perfume.

Tansy, calaminth and daisies,
    On the river's margin thrive;
And accompany the mazes
    Of the stream that leaps alive.

Muse, accordant to the season,
    Give the numbers life and air;
When the sounds and objects reason
    In behalf of praise and pray'r.

All the scenes of nature quicken,
    By the genial spirits fann'd;
And the painted beauties thicken
    Colour'd by the master's hand.

Earth her vigour repossessing
    As the blasts are held in ward;
Blessing heap'd and press'd on blessing,
    Yield the measure of the Lord.

Beeches, without order seemly,
    Shade the flow'rs of annual birth,
And the lily smiles supremely
    Mention'd by the Lord on earth.

Cowslips seize upon the fallow,
    And the cardamine in white,
Where the corn-flow'rs join the mallow,
    Joy and health, and thrift unite.

Study sits beneath her arbour,
    By the bason's glossy side;
While the boat from out its harbour
    Exercise and pleasure guide.

Pray'r and praise be mine employment,
    Without grudging or regret;
Lasting life, and long enjoyment,
    Are not here, and are not yet.

Hark! aloud, the black-bird whistles,
    With surrounding fragrance blest,
And the goldfinch in the thistles
    Makes provision for her nest.

Ev'n the hornet hives his honey,
    Bluecap builds his stately dome,
And the rocks supply the coney
    With a fortress and an home.

But the servants of their Saviour,
    Which with gospel peace are shod,
Have no bed but what the paviour
    Makes them in the porch of God.

O thou house that hold'st the charter
    Of salvation from on high,
Fraught with prophet, saint, and martyr,
    Born to weep, to starve and die!

Great today thy song and rapture
    In the Choir of Christ and WREN
When two prizes were the capture
    Of the hand that fish'd for men.

To the man of quick compliance
    Jesus call'd, and Philip came;
And began to make alliance
    For his master's cause and name.

James, of title most illustrious,
    Brother of the Lord, allow'd;
In the vineyard how industrious,
    Nor by years nor hardship bow'd!

Each accepted in his trial,
    One the CHEERFUL one the JUST;
Both of love and self-denial,
    Both of everlasting trust.

Living they dispens'd salvation,
    Heav'n-endow'd with grace and pow'r;
And they dy'd in imitation
    Of their Saviour's final hour,

Who, for cruel traitors pleading,
    Triumph'd in his parting breath;
O'er all miracles preceding
    His inestimable death.

CHARLES CHURCHILL

from The Times

Go where we will, at every time and place,
Sodom confronts, and stares us in the face;
They ply in public at our very doors,
And take the bread from much more honest whores.
Those who are mean high paramours secure,
And the rich guilty screen the guilty poor;
The sin too proud to feel from reason awe,
And those who practise it too great for law.
    Woman, the pride and happiness of man,
Without whose soft endearments Nature's plan
Had been a blank, and life not worth a thought;
Woman, by all the Loves and Graces taught
With softest arts, and sure, though hidden skill,
To humanise, and mould us to her will;
Woman, with more than common grace form'd here,
With the persuasive language of a tear
To melt the rugged temper of our isle,
Or win us to her purpose with a smile;
Woman, by fate the quickest spur decreed,
The fairest, best reward of every deed
Which bears the stamp of honour; at whose name
Our ancient heroes caught a quicker flame,
And dared beyond belief, whilst o'er the plain,
Spurning the carcases of princes slain,
Confusion proudly strode, whilst Horror blew
The fatal trump, and Death stalk'd full in view;
Woman is out of date, a thing thrown by
As having lost its use: no more the eye,
Gazes entranced, and could for ever gaze;
No more the heart, that seat where Love resides,

Each breath drawn quick and short, in fuller tides
Life posting through the veins, each pulse on fire,
And the whole body tingling with desire,
Pants for those charms, which Virtue might engage
To break his vow, and thaw the frost of Age,
Bidding each trembling nerve, each muscle strain,
And giving pleasure which is almost pain.
Women are kept for nothing but the breed;
For pleasure we must have a Ganymede,
A fine, fresh Hylas, a delicious boy,
To serve our purposes of beastly joy.

[293–334]

GEORGE CRABBE

from Peter Grimes

Peter had heard there were in London then, –
Still have they being! – workhouse-clearing men,
Who, undisturb'd by feelings just or kind,
Would parish-boys to needy tradesmen bind:
They in their want a trifling sum would take,
And toiling slaves of piteous orphans make.

   Such Peter sought, and when a lad was found,
The sum was dealt him, and the slave was bound.
Some few in town observed in Peter's trap
A boy, with jacket blue and woollen cap;
But none inquired how Peter used the rope,
Or what the bruise, that made the stripling stoop;
None could the ridges on his back behold,
None sought him shiv'ring in the winter's cold;
None put the question – 'Peter, dost thou give
The boy his food? – What, man! the lad must live:
Consider, Peter, let the child have bread,
He'll serve thee better if he's stroked and fed.'
None reason'd thus – and some, on hearing cries,
Said calmly, 'Grimes is at his exercise.'

   Pinn'd, beaten, old, pinch'd, threaten'd, and abused –
His efforts punish'd and his food refused, –
Awake tormented, – soon aroused from sleep, –
Struck if he wept, and yet compell'd to weep,
The trembling boy dropp'd down and strove to pray,
Received a blow, and trembling turn'd away,
Or sobb'd and hid his piteous face; – while he,
The savage master, grinn'd in horrid glee:
He'd now the power he ever loved to show,
A feeling being subject to his blow.

Thus lived the lad, in hunger, peril, pain,
His tears despised, his supplications vain:
Compell'd by fear to lie, by need to steal,
His bed uneasy and unbless'd his meal,
For three sad years the boy his tortures bore,
And then his pains and trials were no more.

'How died he, Peter?' when the people said,
He growl'd – 'I found him lifeless in his bed;'
Then tried for softer tone, and sigh'd, 'Poor Sam is dead.'
Yet murmurs were there, and some questions ask'd, –
How he was fed, how punish'd, and how task'd?
Much they suspected, but they little proved,
And Peter pass'd untroubled and unmoved.

Another boy with equal ease was found,
The money granted, and the victim bound;
And what his fate? – One night it chanced he fell
From the boat's mast and perish'd in her well,
Where fish were living kept, and where the boy
(So reason'd men) could not himself destroy: –

'Yes! so it was,' said Peter, 'in his play,
(For he was idle both by night and day,)
He climb'd the main-mast and then fell below;' –
Then show'd the corpse and pointed to the blow:
What said the jury? – they were long in doubt,
But sturdy Peter faced the matter out:
So they dismiss'd him, saying at the time,
'Keep fast your hatchway when you've boys who climb.'
This hit the conscience, and he colour'd more
Than for the closest questions put before.

Thus all his fears the verdict set aside,
And at the slave-shop Peter still applied.

Then came a boy, of manners soft and mild, –
Our seamen's wives with grief beheld the child;
All thought (the poor themselves) that he was one
Of gentle blood, some noble sinner's son,
Who had, belike, deceived some humble maid,

Whom he had first seduced and then betray'd: –
However this, he seem'd a gracious lad,
In grief submissive and with patience sad.
    Passive he labour'd, till his slender frame
Bent with his loads, and he at length was lame:
Strange that a frame so weak could bear so long
The grossest insult and the foulest wrong;
But there were causes – in the town they gave
Fire, food, and comfort, to the gentle slave;
And though stern Peter, with a cruel hand,
And knotted rope, enforced the rude command,
Yet he consider'd what he'd lately felt,
And his vile blows with selfish pity dealt.
    One day such draughts the cruel fisher made,
He could not vend them in his borough-trade,
But sail'd for London-mart: the boy was ill,
But ever humbled to his master's will;
And on the river, where they smoothly sail'd,
He strove with terror and awhile prevail'd;
But new to danger on the angry sea,
He clung affrighten'd to his master's knee:
The boat grew leaky and the wind was strong,
Rough was the passage and the time was long;
His liquor fail'd, and Peter's wrath arose, –
No more is known – the rest we must suppose,
Or learn of Peter; – Peter says, he 'spied
The stripling's danger and for harbour tried;
Meantime the fish, and then th'apprentice died.'

[59–152]

WILLIAM WORDSWORTH

From the Italian of Michael Angelo

No mortal object did these eyes behold
When first they met the placid light of thine,
And my Soul felt her destiny divine,
And hope of endless peace in me grew bold:
Heav'n born, the Soul a heav'n-ward course must hold;
Beyond the visible world She soars to seek,
For what delights the sense is false and weak,
Ideal Form, the universal mould.
The wise man, I affirm, can find no rest
In that which perishes: nor will he lend
His heart to aught which doth on time depend.
'Tis sense, unbridled will, and not true love,
Which kills the soul: Love betters what is best,
Even here below, but more in heaven above.

GEORGE GORDON, LORD BYRON

'When we two parted ... '

When we two parted
    In silence and tears,
Half broken-hearted
    To sever for years,
Pale grew thy cheek and cold,
    Colder thy kiss;
Truly that hour foretold
    Sorrow to this.

The dew of the morning
    Sunk chill on my brow –
It felt like the warning
    Of what I feel now.
Thy vows are all broken,
    And light is thy fame;
I hear thy name spoken,
    And share in its shame.

They name thee before me,
    A knell to mine ear;
A shudder comes o'er me –
    Why wert thou so dear?
They know not I knew thee,
    Who knew thee too well: –
Long, long shall I rue thee,
    Too deeply to tell.

In secret we met –
    In silence I grieve,
That thy heart could forget,
    Thy spirit deceive.
If I should meet thee
    After long years,
How should I greet thee! –
    With silence and tears.

OSCAR WILDE

On the Sale by Auction of Keats' Love Letters

These are the letters which Endymion wrote
  To one he loved in secret, and apart.
  And now the brawlers of the auction mart
Bargain and bid for each poor blotted note,
Ay! for each separate pulse of passion quote
  The merchant's price. I think they love not art
  Who break the crystal of a poet's heart
That small and sickly eyes may glare and gloat.

Is it not said that many years ago,
  In a far Eastern town, some soldiers ran
  With torches through the midnight, and began
To wrangle for mean raiment, and to throw
  Dice for the garments of a wretched man,
Not knowing the God's wonder, or His woe?

WILFRED OWEN

Arms and the Boy

Let the boy try along this bayonet-blade
How cold steel is, and keen with hunger of blood;
Blue with all malice, like a madman's flash;
And thinly drawn with famishing for flesh.

Lend him to stroke these blind, blunt bullet-leads
Which long to nuzzle in the hearts of lads,
Or give him cartridges of fine zinc teeth,
Sharp with the sharpness of grief and death.

For his teeth seem for laughing round an apple.
There lurk no claws behind his fingers supple;
And God will grow no talons at his heels,
Nor antlers through the thickness of his curls.

VI IN MEMORIAM

The elegy, like the pastoral, is one of gay love poetry's oldest disguises. It is easy to see why: the great epic poems of Homer and Virgil, in recording the heroic events of their nations' wars, naturally celebrate male friendships and mourn their violent ends in battle. So we have Achilles' grief following the death of his lover Patroclus in *The Iliad*; and, from *The Aeneid*, the deaths of Euryalus and Nisus, with Virgil's own memorializing intervention – a formula exactly echoed in the eighteenth of Shakespeare's sonnets, which begins with hyperbolic praise of the loved one's beauty but ends with a rather smug (and, of course, absolutely correct) assertion of the memorial poem's ability to outlast it.

To anyone who thinks of Tennyson as a pompous and somewhat ludicrous Victorian, reading or re-reading *In Memoriam* is likely to come as a shock: I've included a mere half-dozen sections from this magnificently sustained poem, which is startlingly honest and not at all bombastic. Walt Whitman's great elegy 'When Lilacs Last in the Dooryard Bloom'd' is an almost contemporary but very different affair, which should prove no less surprising to readers who think they don't like Whitman.

The twentieth-century elegies here include poems – by Wilfred Owen and J.R. Ackerley – from both world wars. But the overwhelming occasion for gay elegiac writing in the late twentieth century is inescapably AIDS: I have included several such pieces and could easily have found many more, but even – or especially – these are celebrations too. That is why it seems absolutely right to end the book with Adam Johnson's 'The Playground Bell', a self-elegizing poem which quite marvellously reaffirms its dying author's utterly undiminished relish for life.

HOMER
Translated by Alexander Pope

from The Iliad

Thus like the rage of fire the combat burns,
And now it rises, now it sinks by turns.
Meanwhile, where Hellespont's broad waters flow,
Stood Nestor's son, the messenger of woe:
There sat Achilles, shaded by his sails,
On hoisted yards extended to the gales;
Pensive he sat; for all that fate design'd
Rose in sad prospect to his boding mind.
Thus to his soul he said: 'Ah! what constrains
The Greeks, late victors, now to quit the plains?
Is this the day, which heaven so long ago
Ordain'd, to sink me with the weight of woe?
(So Thetis warn'd;) when by a Trojan hand
The bravest of the Myrmidonian band
Should lose the light! Fulfilled is that decree;
Fallen is the warrior, and Patroclus he!
In vain I charged him soon to quit the plain,
And warn'd to shun Hectorean force in vain!'
     Thus while he thinks, Antilochus appears,
And tells the melancholy tale with tears.
'Sad tidings, son of Peleus! thou must hear;
And wretched I, the unwilling messenger!
Dead is Patroclus! For his corse they fight;
His naked corse: his arms are Hector's right.'
     A sudden horror shot through all the chief,
And wrapp'd his senses in the cloud of grief;
Cast on the ground, with furious hands he spread
The scorching ashes o'er his graceful head;
His purple garments, and his golden hairs,
These he deforms with dust, and these he tears;
On the hard soil his groaning breast he threw,

And roll'd and grovell'd, as to earth he grew.
The virgin captives, with disorder'd charms,
(Won by his own, or by Patroclus' arms,)
Rush'd from their tents with cries; and gathering round,
Beat their white breasts, and fainted on the ground:
While Nestor's son sustains a manlier part,
And mourns the warrior with a warrior's heart;
Hangs on his arms, amidst his frantic woe,
And oft prevents the meditated blow.

   [XVIII: 1–40]

   He, deeply groaning – 'To this cureless grief,
Not even the Thunderer's favour brings relief.
Patroclus – Ah! – say, goddess, can I boast
A pleasure now? revenge itself is lost;
Patroclus, loved of all my martial train,
Beyond mankind, beyond myself, is slain!
Lost are those arms the gods themselves bestow'd
On Peleus; Hector bears the glorious load.
Cursed be that day, when all the powers above
Thy charms submitted to a mortal love:
O hadst thou still, a sister of the main,
Pursued the pleasures of the watery reign:
And happier Peleus, less ambitious, led
A mortal beauty to his equal bed!
Ere the sad fruit of thy unhappy womb
Had caused such sorrows past, and woes to come.
For soon, alas! that wretched offspring slain,
New woes, new sorrows, shall create again.
'Tis not in fate the alternate now to give;
Patroclus dead, Achilles hates to live.
Let me revenge it on proud Hector's heart,
Let his last spirit smoke upon my dart;
On these conditions will I breathe: till then,
I blush to walk among the race of men.'

   [XVIII: 99–122]

VIRGIL

Translated by John Dryden

from The Aeneid

Fierce Volscens foams with rage, and gazing round,
Descried not him who gave the deadly wound,
Nor knew to fix revenge: 'But thou (he cries),
Shalt pay for both,' and at the prisoner flies
With his drawn sword. Then, struck with deep despair,
That cruel sight the lover could not bear;
But from his covert rushed in open view.
And sent his voice before him as he flew:
'Me! me! (he cried) turn all your swords alone
On me – the fact confessed, the fault my own.
He neither could nor durst, the guiltless youth –
Ye moon and stars, bear witness to the truth!
His only crime (if friendship can offend)
Is too much love of his unhappy friend.'
Too late he speaks: the sword, which fury guides,
Driven with full force, had pierced his tender sides.
Down fell the beauteous youth: the yawning wound
Gushed out a purple stream, and stained the ground.
His snowy neck reclines upon his breast,
Like a fair flower by the keen share oppressed –
Like a white poppy sinking on the plain,
Whose heavy head is overcharged with rain.

    Despair, and rage, and vengeance justly vowed,
Drove Nisus headlong on the hostile crowd.
Volscens he seeks; and him alone he bends:
Borne back and bored by his surrounding friends,
Onward he pressed, and kept him still in sight,
Then whirled aloft his sword with all his might:
The unerring steel descended while he spoke,

Pierced his wide mouth, and through his weazon broke.
Dying, he slew; and staggering on the plain,
With swimming eyes he sought his lover slain;
Then quiet on his bleeding bosom fell,
Content, in death, to be revenged so well.
    O happy friends! for, if my verse can give
Immortal life, your fame shall ever live,
Fixed as the Capitol's foundation lies,
And spread where'er the Roman eagle flies!

[IX: 421–458]

MICHAEL DRAYTON

from Piers Gaveston

O break my heart, quoth he, O break and die,
Whose infant thoughts were nursed with sweet delight;
But now the inn of care and misery,
Whose pleasing hope is murdered with despight:
    O end my days, for now my joys are done,
    Wanting my Piers, my sweetest Gaveston.

Farewell my love, companion of my youth,
My soul's delight, the subject of my mirth,
My second self if I report the truth,
The rare and only phoenix of the earth,
    Farewell sweet friend, with thee my joys are gone,
    Farewell my Piers, my lovely Gaveston.

What are the rest but painted imagery,
Dumb idols made to fill up idle rooms,
But gaudy antics, sports of foolery,
But fleshly coffins, goodly gilded tombs,
    But puppets which with others' words reply,
    Like prattling echoes soothing every lie?

O damnèd world, I scorn thee and thy worth,
The very source of all iniquity:
An ugly dam that brings such monsters forth,
The maze of death, nurse of impiety,
    A filthy sink, where loathsomeness doth dwell,
    A labyrinth, a gaol, a very hell.

Deceitful siren traitor to my youth,
Bane to my bliss, false thief that steal'st my joys:
Mother of lies, sworn enemy to truth,
The ship of fools fraught all with gauds and toys,
    A vessel stuffed with foul hypocrisy,
    The very temple of idolatry.

O earth-pale Saturn most malevolent,
Combustious planet, tyrant in thy reign,
The sword of wrath, the root of discontent,
In whose ascendant all my joys are slain:
    Thou executioner of foul bloody rage,
    To act the will of lame decrepit age.

My life is but a very map of woes,
My joys the fruit of an untimely birth,
My youth in labour with unkindly throws,
My pleasures are like plagues that rain on earth,
    All my delights like streams that swiftly run,
    Or like the dew exhalèd by the sun.

    [469–510]

WILLIAM SHAKESPEARE

Sonnet 18

Shall I compare thee to a summer's day?
Thou art more lovely and more temperate.
Rough winds do shake the darling buds of May,
And summer's lease hath all too short a date.
Sometime too hot the eye of heaven shines,
And often is his gold complexion dimmed;
And every fair from fair sometime declines,
By chance, or nature's changing course, untrimmed;
But thy eternal summer shall not fade,
Nor lose possession of that fair thou ow'st,
Nor shall Death brag thou wand'rest in his shade,
When in eternal lines to time thou grow'st.
    So long as men can breathe or eyes can see,
    So long lives this, and this gives life to thee.

THOMAS GRAY

Sonnet on the Death of Mr Richard West

In vain to me the smiling mornings shine,
And reddening Phoebus lifts his golden fire:
The birds in vain their amorous descant join,
Or cheerful fields resume their green attire:
These ears, alas! for other notes repine,
A different object do these eyes require.
My lonely anguish melts no heart but mine;
And in my breast the imperfect joys expire.
Yet morning smiles the busy race to cheer,
And new-born pleasure brings to happier men:
The fields to all their wonted tribute bear;
To warm their little loves the birds complain.
I fruitless mourn to him that cannot hear,
And weep the more because I weep in vain.

ALFRED, LORD TENNYSON

from In Memoriam A.H.H.

VII

Dark house, by which once more I stand
    Here in the long unlovely street,
    Doors, where my heart was used to beat
So quickly, waiting for a hand,

A hand that can be clasp'd no more –
    Behold me, for I cannot sleep,
    And like a guilty thing I creep
At earliest morning to the door.

He is not here; but far away
    The noise of life begins again,
    And ghastly thro' the drizzling rain
On the bald street breaks the blank day.

XXVII

I envy not in any moods
    The captive void of noble rage,
    The linnet born within the cage,
That never knew the summer woods:

I envy not the beast that takes
    His license in the field of time,
    Unfetter'd by the sense of crime,
To whom a conscience never wakes;

Nor, what may count itself as blest,
    The heart that never plighted troth
    But stagnates in the weeds of sloth;
Nor any want-begotten rest.

I hold it true, whate'er befall;
    I feel it, when I sorrow most;
    'Tis better to have loved and lost
Than never to have loved at all.

L

Be near me when my light is low,
    When the blood creeps, and the nerves prick
    And tingle; and the heart is sick,
And all the wheels of Being slow.

Be near me when the sensuous frame
    Is rack'd with pangs that conquer trust;
    And Time, a maniac scattering dust,
And Life, a Fury slinging flame.

Be near me when my faith is dry,
    And men the flies of latter spring,
    That lay their eggs, and sting and sing
And weave their petty cells and die.

Be near me when I fade away,
    To point the term of human strife,
    And on the low dark verge of life
The twilight of eternal day.

LXXXI

Could I have said while he was here,
   'My love shall now no further range;
   There cannot come a mellower change,
For now is love mature in ear.'

Love, then, had hope of richer store:
   What end is here to my complaint?
   This haunting whisper makes me faint,
'More years had made me love thee more.'

But Death returns an answer sweet:
   'My sudden frost was sudden gain,
   And gave all ripeness to the grain,
It might have drawn from after-heat.'

CXXIX

Dear friend, far off, my lost desire,
   So far, so near in woe and weal;
   O loved the most, when most I feel
There is a lower and a higher;

Known and unknown; human, divine;
   Sweet human hand and lips and eye;
   Dear heavenly friend that canst not die,
Mine, mine, for ever, ever mine;

Strange friend, past, present, and to be;
   Loved deeplier, darklier understood;
   Behold, I dream a dream of good,
And mingle all the world with thee.

CXXX

Thy voice is on the rolling air;
   I hear thee where the waters run;
   Thou standest in the rising sun,
And in the setting thou art fair.

What art thou then? I cannot guess;
   But tho' I seem in star and flower
   To feel thee some diffusive power,
I do not therefore love thee less:

My love involves the love before;
   My love is vaster passion now;
   Tho' mix'd with God and Nature thou,
I seem to love thee more and more.

Far off thou art, but ever nigh;
   I have thee still, and I rejoice;
   I prosper, circled with thy voice;
I shall not lose thee tho' I die.

WALT WHITMAN

When Lilacs Last in the Dooryard Bloom'd

I

When lilacs last in the dooryard bloom'd,
And the great star early dropp'd in the western sky in the night,
I mourn'd, and yet shall mourn with ever-returning spring.

Ever-returning spring, trinity sure to me you bring,
Lilac blooming perennial and drooping star in the west,
And thought of him I love.

2

O powerful western fallen star!
O shades of night – O moody, tearful night!
O great star disappear'd – O the black murk that hides the star!
O cruel hands that hold me powerless – O helpless soul of me!
O harsh surrounding cloud that will not free my soul.

3

In the dooryard fronting an old farm-house near the white-
    wash'd palings,
Stands the lilac-bush tall-growing with heart-shaped leaves
    of rich green,
With many a pointed blossom rising delicate, with the
    perfume strong I love,
With every leaf a miracle – and from this bush in the
    dooryard,
With delicate-color'd blossoms and heart-shaped leaves
    of rich green,
A sprig with its flower I break.

4

In the swamp in secluded recesses,
A shy and hidden bird is warbling a song.
Solitary the thrush,
The hermit withdrawn to himself, avoiding the settlements,
Sings by himself a song.

Song of the bleeding throat,
Death's outlet song of life, (for well dear brother I know,
If thou wast not granted to sing thou would'st surely die.)

5

Over the breast of the spring, the land, amid cities,
Amid lanes and through old woods, where lately the violet's
   peep'd from the ground, spotting the gray debris,
Amid the grass in the fields each side of the lanes, passing
   the endless grass,
Passing the yellow-spear'd wheat, every grain from its shroud
   in the dark-brown fields uprisen,
Passing the apple-tree blows of white and pink in the orchards,
Carrying a corpse to where it shall rest in the grave,
Night and day journeys a coffin.

6

Coffin that passes through lanes and streets,
Through day and night with the great cloud darkening
   the land,
With the pomp of the inloop'd flags with the cities
   draped in black,
With the show of the States themselves as of crape-veil'd
   women standing,
With processions long and winding and the flambeaus
   of the night,

With the countless torches lit, with the silent sea of faces
    and the unbared heads,
With the waiting depot, the arriving coffin, and the sombre
    faces,
With dirges through the night, with the thousand voices
    rising strong and solemn,
With all the mournful voices of the dirges pour'd around
    the coffin,
The dim-lit churches and the shuddering organs – where amid
    these you journey,
With the tolling tolling bells' perpetual clang,
Here, coffin that slowly passes,
I give you my sprig of lilac.

7

(Not for you, for one alone,
Blossoms and branches green to coffins all I bring,
For fresh as the morning, thus would I chant a song for you
    O sane and sacred death.

All over bouquets of roses,
O death, I cover you over with roses and early lilies,
But mostly and now the lilac that blooms the first,
Copious I break, I break the sprigs from the bushes,
With loaded arms I come, pouring for you,
For you and the coffins all of you O death.)

8

O western orb sailing the heaven,
Now as I know what you must have meant as a month
    since I walk'd,
As I saw you had something to tell as you bent to me
    night after night,
As you droop'd from the sky low down as if to my side,
    (while the other stars all look'd on,)

As we wander'd together the solemn night, (for something
I know not what kept me from sleep,)
As the night advances, and I saw on the rim of the west
how full you were of woe,
As I stood on the rising ground in the breeze in the cool
transparent night,
As I watch'd where you pass'd and was lost in the netherward
black of the night,
As my soul in its trouble dissatisfied sank, as where
you sad orb,
Concluded, dropt in the night, and was gone.

9

Sing on there in the swamp,
O singer bashful and tender, I hear your notes, I hear your call,
I hear, I come presently, I understand you,
But a moment I linger, for the lustrous star has detain'd me,
The star my despairing comrade holds and detains me.

10

O how shall I warble myself for the dead one there I loved?
And how shall I deck my song for the large sweet soul
that has gone?
And what shall my perfume be for the grave of him I love?
Sea-winds blown from east and west,
Blown from the Eastern sea and blown from the Western sea,
till there on the prairies meeting,
These and with these and the breath of my chant,
I'll perfume the grave of him I love.

11

O what shall I hang on the chamber walls?
And what shall the pictures be that I hang on the walls,
To adorn the burial-house of him I love?

Pictures of growing spring and farms and homes,
With the Fourth-month eve at sundown, and the gray smoke
    lucid and bright,
With floods of the yellow gold of the gorgeous, indolent,
    sinking sun, burning, expanding the air,
With the fresh sweet herbage under foot, and the pale green
    leaves of the trees prolific,
In the distance the flowing glaze, the breast of the river,
    with a wind-dapple here and there,
With ranging hills on the banks, with many a line against
    the sky, and shadows,
And the city at hand with dwellings so dense, and stacks
    of chimneys,
And all the scenes of life and the workshops, and the workmen
    homeward returning.

12

Lo, body and soul – this land,
My own Manhattan with spires, and the sparkling and
    hurrying tides, and the ships,
The varied and ample land, the South and the North in the
    light, Ohio's shores and flashing Missouri,
And ever the far-spreading prairies cover'd with grass and corn.
Lo, the most excellent sun so calm and haughty,
The violet and purple morn with just-felt breezes,
The gentle soft-born measureless light
The miracle spreading bathing all, the fulfill'd noon,
The coming eve delicious, the welcome night and the stars,
Over my cities shining all, enveloping man and land.

13

Sing on, sing on you gray-brown bird,
Sing from the swamps, the recesses, pour your chant
    from the bushes,
Limitless out of the dusk, out of the cedars and pines.

Sing on dearest brother, warble your reedy song,
Loud human song, with voice of utmost woe.
O liquid and free and tender!
O wild and loose to my soul – O wondrous singer!
You only I hear – yet the star holds me, (but will soon depart,)
Yet the lilac with mastering odour holds me.

14

Now while I sat in the day and look'd forth,
In the close of the day with its light and the fields of spring,
    and the farmers preparing their crops,
In the large unconscious scenery of my land with its lakes
    and forests,
In the heavenly aerial beauty, (after the perturb'd winds
    and the storms,)
Under the arching heavens of the afternoon swift passing,
    and the voices of children and women,
The many-moving sea-tides, and I saw the ships how they
    sail'd,
And the summer approaching with richness, and the fields
    all busy with labour,
And the infinite separate houses, how they all went on,
    each with its meals and minutiae of daily usages,
And the streets how their throbbings throbb'd, and the cities
    pent – lo, then and there,
Falling upon them all and among them all, enveloping me
    with the rest,
Appear'd the cloud, appear'd the long black trail,
And I knew death, its thought, and the sacred knowledge
    of death.

Then with the knowledge of death as walking one side of me,
And the thought of death close-walking the other side of me,
And I in the middle as with companions, and as holding
    the hands of companions,
I fled forth to the hiding receiving night that talks not,

Down to the shores of the water, the path by the swamp
    in the dimness,
To the solemn shadowy cedars and ghostly pines so still.

And the singer so shy to the rest receiv'd me,
The gray-brown bird I know receiv'd us comrades three,
And he sang the carol of death, and a verse for him I love.

From deep secluded recesses,
From the fragrant cedars and the ghostly pines so still,
Came the carol of the bird.

And the charm of the carol rapt me,
As I held as if by their hands my comrades in the night,
And the voices of my spirit tallied the song of the bird.

Come lovely and soothing death,
Undulate round the world, serenely arriving, arriving,
In the day, in the night, to all, to each,
Sooner or later delicate death.

Prais'd be the fathomless universe,
For life and joy, and for objects and knowledge curious,
And for love, sweet love – but praise! praise! praise!
For the sure-enwinding arms of cool-enfolding death.

Dark mother always gliding near with soft feet,
Have none chanted for thee a chant of fullest welcome?
Then I chant it for thee, I glorify thee above all,
I bring thee a song that when thou must indeed come,
    come unfalteringly.

Approach strong deliveress,
When it is so, when thou hast taken them I joyously sing the dead,
Lost in the loving floating ocean of thee,
Laved in the flood of thy bliss O death.

From me to thee glad serenades,
Dances for thee I propose saluting thee, adornments and feastings
    for thee,
And the sights of the open landscape and the high-spread sky
    are fitting,
And life and the fields, and the huge and thoughtful night.

The night in silence under many a star,
The ocean shore and the husky whispering wave whose voice
    I know,
And the soul turning to thee O vast and well-veil'd death,
And the body gratefully nestling close to thee.

Over the tree-tops I float thee a song,
Over the rising and sinking waves, over the myriad fields
    and the prairies wide,
Over the dense-pack'd cities all and the teeming wharves
    and ways,
I float this carol with joy, with joy to thee O death.

15

To the tally of my soul,
Loud and strong kept up the gray-brown bird,
With pure deliberate notes spreading filling the night.

Loud in the pines and cedars dim,
Clear in the freshness moist and the swamp-perfume,
And I with my comrades there in the night.

While my sight that was bound in my eyes unclosed,
As to long panoramas of visions.

And I saw askant the armies,
I saw as in noiseless dreams hundreds of battle-flags,
Borne through the smoke of the battles and pierc'd
    with missiles I saw them,

And carried hither and yon through the smoke, and torn
   and bloody,
And at last but a few shreds left on the staffs, (and all in
   silence,)
And the staffs all splinter'd and broken.

I saw battle-corpses, myriads of them,
And the white skeletons of young men, I saw them,
I saw the debris and debris of all the slain soldiers of the war,
But I saw they were not as was thought,
They themselves were fully at rest, they suffer'd not,
The living remain'd and suffer'd, the mother suffer'd,
And the wife and the child and the musing comrade suffer'd,
And the armies that remain'd suffer'd.

16

Passing the visions, passing the night,
Passing, unloosing the hold of my comrades' hands,
Passing the song of the hermit bird and the tallying song
   of my soul,
Victorious song, death's outlet song, yet varying ever-altering
   song,
As low and wailing, yet clear the notes, rising and falling,
   flooding the night,
Sadly sinking and fainting, as warning and warning,
   and yet again bursting with joy,
Covering the earth and filling the spread of the heaven,
As that powerful psalm in the night I heard from recesses,
Passing, I leave thee lilac with heart-shaped leaves,
I leave thee there in the door-yard, blooming, returning with
   spring.

I cease from my song for thee,
From my gaze on thee in the west, fronting the west,
   communing with thee,
O comrade lustrous with silver face in the night.

Yet each to keep and all, retrievements out of the night,
The song, the wondrous chant of the gray-brown bird,
And the tallying chant, the echo arous'd in my soul,
With the lustrous and drooping star with the countenance
    full of woe,
With the holders holding my hand nearing the call of the bird,
Comrades mine and I in the midst, and their memory ever to
    keep, for the dead I loved so well,
For the sweetest, wisest soul of all my days and lands – and this
    for his dear sake,
Lilac and star and bird twined with the chant of my soul,
There in the fragrant pines and the cedars dusk and dim.

PAUL VERLAINE
Translated by Mark Beech

from Lucien Létinois

You were not in my arms when you died,
Though it seemed that you were, for your pain
And your boundless distress were both shared.
Delirious, paler than linen,

You held me instead with your voice,
Saying sweet wild things – 'I was dead,
It was sad' – and you gripped tight my hand
As you stared into infinite space.

I turned, trembling, to cover my tears,
While you in your fever continued
To talk and to call out my name:
Then, grief beyond grief, it was over.

I ought to have died in your place
As you stood there waving goodbye ...
And now there is no more to say,
But pardon, just God, my audacity.

WILFRED OWEN

Fragment: I saw his round mouth's crimson ...

I saw his round mouth's crimson deepen as it fell,
    Like a Sun, in his last deep hour;
Watched the magnificent recession of farewell,
    Clouding, half gleam, half glower,
And a last splendour burn the heavens of his cheek.
    And in his eyes
The cold stars lighting, very old and bleak,
    In different skies.

J.R. ACKERLEY

Missing
To F.H.

We never knew what became of him, that was so curious;
He embarked, it was late in November, and never returned;
No time for farewells and the journey so far and precarious;
A few letters reached us long after and came to an end.

The weeks lingered on into months and again to November;
We troubled the officials, of course, and they cabled about,
They were patient but busy, importunities without number;
Some told us one thing, some another, they never found out.

There's a lot go like that, I suppose, with no explanation,
And death is death, after all, small comfort to know where
          and when;
But I keep thinking, now that we've dropped the investigation:
It was more like the death of an insect than that of a man.

This beetle, for instance; I lower my boot now to crush it,
And who's to correct me, correct me? Who is to know?
I do not ask whether the other beetles will miss it,
Or God will say 'Where is my beetle? Where did it go?'

The life and the tiny delight, the sublime fabrication
Of colour, mechanics and form, I care nothing about;
I a man with his mind, the master, the lord of creation;
This beetle impedes me, offends me, I lower my boot.

And that was the way that he went. Yes, I see the rejoinder:
He was one of us, bound with us, shod with the violence
 and pride
Of man in his militant madness, of man the contender ...
But he was my friend and that was the way that he died.

JOHN HEATH-STUBBS

In Memory

A scruffy beer drinkers' club, a basement
In a side street off the Charing Cross Road –
No introductions, and no names exchanged.
And then my room, a cellar
Under the pavement, near Lancaster Gate.
He spoke of the outback, of Ned Kelly –
A wild colonial boy with do-it-yourself armour –
Reproached me for my self-indulgent guilt.
'Nailed upon your private cross,' he said.
And, after that – it was not satisfactory:
Neither of us exactly young – for him
Only the second time with another man, he told me.

But, later on, I recognized
(I was in America) his photo
Upon the cover of a magazine.
Unmistakable the balding head,
The battered face, broad shouldered stocky body.
I wondered if we'd ever meet again,
And if we did by chance, would he remember,
Or take it as a threat? But that
Was three decades ago and some years more.
And now a voice upon the air-waves tells me
That he is gone. He's dead and celebrated,
And then they played an interview
Recorded some years back. But residence
In England had quite sandpapered away
All the Australian vowels. But I am grieving –
Grieving for a little twig of love
That never blossomed – could not, should not blossom,
Among the debris of my journey's sidewalk.

THOM GUNN

In the Post Office

Saw someone yesterday who looked like you did,
Being short with long blond hair, a sturdy kid
Ahead of me in line. I gazed and gazed
At his good back, feeling again, amazed,
That almost envious sexual tension which
Rubbing at made the greater, like an itch,
An itch to steal or otherwise possess
The brilliant restive charm, the boyishness
That half aware – and not aware enough –
Of what it did, eluded to hold off
The very push of interest it begot,
As if you'd been a tease, though you were not.
I hadn't felt it roused, to tell the truth,
In several years, that old man's greed for youth,
Like Pelias's that boiled him to a soup,
Not since I'd had the sense to cover up
My own particular seething can of worms,
And settle for a friendship on your terms.

Meanwhile I had to look: his errand done,
Without a glance at me or anyone,
The kid unlocked his bicycle outside,
Shrugging a backpack on. I watched him ride
Down 18th Street, rising above the saddle
For the long plunge he made with every pedal,
Expending far more energy than needed.
If only I could do whatever he did,
With him or as part of him, if I
Could creep into his armpit like a fly,
Or like a crab cling to his golden crotch,
Instead of having to stand back and watch.

Oh complicated fantasy of intrusion
On that young sweaty body. My confusion
Led me at length to recollections of
Another's envy and his confused love.

That Fall after you died I went again
To where I had visited you in your pain
But this time for your – friend, roommate, or wooer?
I seek a neutral term where I'm unsure.
He lay there now. Figuring she knew best,
I came by at his mother's phoned request
To pick up one of your remembrances,
A piece of stained-glass you had made, now his,
I did not even remember, far less want.
To him I felt, likewise, indifferent.

'You can come in now,' said the friend-as-nurse.
I did, and found him altered for the worse.
But when he saw me sitting by his bed,
He would not speak, and turned away his head.
I had not known he hated me until
He hated me this much, hated me still.
I thought that we had shared you more or less,
As if we shared what no one might possess,
Since in a net we sought to hold the wind.
There he lay on the pillow, mortally thinned,
Weaker than water, yet his gesture proving
As steady as an undertow. Unmoving,
In the sustained though slight aversion, grim
In wordlessness. Nothing deflected him,
Nothing I did and nothing I could say.
And so I left. I heard he died next day.

I have imagined that he still could taste
That bitterness and anger to the last,
Against the roles he saw me in because

He had to: of victor, as he thought I was,
Of heir, as to the cherished property
His mother – who knows why? – was giving me,
And of survivor, as I am indeed,
Recording, so that I may later read
Of what has happened, whether between sheets,
Or in post offices, or on the streets.

Post Script: The Panel

Reciprocation from the dead. Having finished the post-office
poem, I think I will take a look at the stained-glass panel it
refers to, which C made I would say two years before he died.
I fish it out from where I have kept it, between a filing cabinet
and a small chest of drawers. It has acquired a cobweb, which
I brush off before I look at it. In the lower foreground are a
face with oriental features and an arm, as of someone lying on
his stomach: a mysteriously tiered cone lies behind and above
him. What I had forgotten is that the picture is surrounded on
all four sides by the following inscription:

> The needs of ghosts embarrass the living. A ghost must eat
> and shit, must pack his body someplace. Neither buyer nor
> bundle, a ghost has no tally, no readjusting value, no soul
> counted at a bank.

Is this an excerpt from some Chinese book of wisdom, or is it
C himself speaking? When he made the panel, C may have
already suspected he had AIDS, but the prescience of the first
sentence astonishes me – as it does also that I remembered
nothing of the inscription while writing the poem but looked
it up immediately on finishing it.

Yes, the needs of him and his friend to 'embarrass' me after
their deaths. The dead have no sense of tact, no manners, they
enter doors without knocking, but I continue to deal with
them, as proved by my writing the poem. They pack their
bodies into my dreams, they eat my feelings, and shit in my

mind. They are no good to me, of no value to me, but I cannot shake them and do not want to. Their story, being part of mine, refuses to reach an end. They present me with new problems, surprise me, contradict me, my dear, my everpresent dead.

NEIL POWELL

Hundred River

In memory of Adam Johnson 1965–93

We came to Hundred River through a slow October,
        when earth is scented with everybody's past;
when late scabbed blackberries harden into devil's scars,
        untasted apples rot to bitter toffee.

Across reed-beds a track of blackened railway-sleepers,
        a plank-bridge lapped by barely-stirring water;
swans gargling silently in their fine indifference;
        above, a sky of urgent discursive geese.

Now the year has turned again and I am alone here,
        where willow-herb's dry white whiskers drift over
the brick-red spikes of sorrel and the gossiping reeds;
        and the river sullen, muddied after rain.

No movement in the woods but stealthy growth of fungus,
        hesitant leaf-drop, distant scuttle of deer:
in one marbled, stained oak-leaf I sense gigantic change,
        and in the drizzle feel the season fracture.

STEVE CRANFIELD

Give Me Back My Man

In memoriam Ricky Wilson

I have a secret love. My heart is burning.
But will he play the game? I know some tricks.
I'll fall into his strong arms like a fix.
I'll stir some unmet, deep, unconscious yearning
In his man's breast. Passion will mount. Tides turning.
His swelling manhood pressed. To mine. Limbs mix.
He'll see the light. (I've known since I was six.)
All parts rhyme. Yearning, burning and returning.
Surrendering the all I have to give.
I've got you under my skin. Now each day's
Dawning will bring discoveries, new ways
To mesh us. Never split. Infinitive.
Vows, hearts exchanged. We'll die of love. Clichés,
Like viruses, need our fresh blood to live.

ROBERT COCHRANE

A Private View

for Andrew Heard

It was a day like yesterday
we left the crowd behind,
a day of rare sun
and clean breezes
on the balcony above the river,
and I recall the rise below
of children's voices.
It seemed private.
I'd sensed small clues,
odd details in mail,
our voices within wire,
and you were suddenly thinner.
Skirting the subject,
blaming overwrought concern
I mentioned a friend's mother
almost died of pneumonia,
but you said blankly
'Mine is a very special kind.'
The bomb and the penny fell.
I just hugged you.
Loss of hope at times
stalls the urge to cry
and in the face of your brave one,
mine said nothing.
You said things I'd read,
heard from interviews.
'Not accepting it as terminal.
Fighting this.'

Desperate,
I conjured with
names of long survivors,
but you cut through
'At what cost though?'
From all the words
in my world of them
I could muster none,
my mind reeling
at such savage progress.
Distant from the crowd,
these fragments of exchange
felt personal,
unseen,
but some months
since your funeral,
a friend met there
recalled our exit
from the gallery.
His asking who I was.
Her informative reply.
They watched us
in the distance
like some silent film,
and as I hugged you
she turned to say
'I think he's told him.'

JOEL LANE

Michel Foucault

Your illness was bad enough. The frantic
rush to finish that last book
when the work could never be finished.
All your life, you'd wanted to be a chisel

and not a statue. You'd struck history
at an angle, exposing the fault lines;
always leaning, because the world
was tilted. Pleasure came late,

peace never at all. You were locked back
in your first prison, 'the black stone
of the body' – passive, inscribed
with the stigmata of someone else's

knowledge. The chisels of loss
took your resistance – then chipped away
the shells, one skin at a time. Prayer
and sweat, a damaged being; the things

you went to California to escape.
Full circle. Just as you'd written it:
how the human clay was mass-formed
in factories, schools, prisons, hospitals;

in the confession box, on the couch.
Did you guess how you'd be reborn
as an Icarus on the point of falling –
a postmodern icon, made up of dots

on a screen, revelations on a glossy page?
All the private details: the handcuffs,
the molten wax? Hacks consigned you
to the prison of the flashbulb. A fuck

doesn't merit death or facile celebrity.
But you always knew. There's no place
called freedom. Only these words, these
movements; a level exchange of glances.

ADAM JOHNSON

The Playground Bell

Dead drunk by nine – this used to be enough.
In Manchester I went out every night;
Picked up and stayed wherever there was drink
With men whose names were last thing on my mind –
Including one who slung the Union Jack
Over his bedside lamp for atmosphere
On the Last Night of the Proms in eighty-two;
My first 'experience': even the white socks
I'd been advised to wear were a success –
One foot displayed, half-casually, to mark
My absolute virginity. The final touch:
My mother fixed a blow-wave in my hair.

Always indulgent towards her only son
(Lucky for me my parents got divorced),
She must have sensed I wasn't the same boy
Who'd walked for twenty miles or more a day
On gritstone tracks, over the backs of hills –
The Pennine wastes of Bleaklow, Kinder Scout.

The landscape of the city was more harsh:
Bleaker than any tract of mountain peat,
The bus ride down the Manchester Old Road.
In Sackville Street, between the Thomson's Arms
And the Rembrandt Hotel, a universe
Peopled by drunks and rent boys – one a punk,
Who used to leave his girlfriend at the bar
On business. After barely half an hour,
He'd stroll back in and stand them both a drink.

I quickly learned the language and the code –
Had 'sisters' who were kind men twice my age,
Who paid for beers and thought I was mature;
Confided, gave advice and lent me fares.
On Saturday nights we'd drive to Liverpool
Or Stoke-on-Trent, as if there were a difference
Between one seedy night-spot and another –
Though local accents used to turn me on,
And that rare prize – a genuine foreigner
On holiday, was worth the taxi ride
To some remote hotel. Leaving in secret,
Before breakfast, pocketing an address
(In Paris!) I would never write to, a poignant act.

One Christmas I saved up and went to Heaven –
The biggest dive in England, under Charing Cross –
A three-tiered circuit ranged by packs of men,
And boys who came to dance. I ended up
In a basement somewhere off the Chepstow Road,
And woke to the first snow-fall of the year.
I came to London for a long weekend
And stayed; met someone famous who was kind,
And took a boring job in Portland Place.
I went, on summer nights, to Hampstead Heath,
Where pints of beer at Jack Straw's Castle gave
To sex under the tents of holly trees –
Shadows of hands that flowered through the dusk:
No names, no contracts, but each parting hug
Was less a token of civility
Than an act of love.
                              Later, in Amsterdam,
In crowded cellars on the Warmoesstraat,
The rules were different – a more serious art,
Practised in uniform. The smell of leather
An aphrodisiac keen as the scent of leaves;

And still, the magic of indifference.
It still goes on – wherever hands can find
Response of hands; hold, in the hollow silence,
A tangible warmth, the heartbeat in the dark
Where death has entered, ringing the playground bell.
It hurts the ear. It echoes through the woods.

I stare at death in a mirror behind the bar
And wonder when I sacrificed my blood,
And how I could not recognize the face
That smiled with the mouth, the eyes, of death –
In Manchester, London or Amsterdam.
I do not hate that face, only the bell.

NOTES ON POETS

J.R. ACKERLEY's books include *Hindoo Holiday* (1932), *My Dog Tulip* (1956), *We Think the World of You* (1960) and the posthumously published memoir *My Father and Myself* (1968). He was Literary Editor of *The Listener* from 1935 to 1959.

MARC ALMOND is a singer best known for his recordings with Soft Cell, including 'Tainted Love' (1980).

STEVE ANTHONY, a Gregory Award winner in 1987, edited *Of Eros and of Dust* (1992) and co-edited *Jugular Defences* (1994) with Peter Daniels.

JOHN ASH is the author of *The Goodbyes* (1982), *The Branching Stairs* (1984), *Disbelief* (1987) and *The Burnt Pages* (1991). His *Selected Poems* appeared in 1996. He was born in Manchester, but has spent most of the past decade in New York.

C.P. CAVAFY is one of the most celebrated and influential of modern Greek poets; he spent most of his life in Alexandria, the city inextricably associated with his work.

ROBERT COCHRANE, born in Ireland, now lives in Manchester where he runs The Bad Press.

STEVE CRANFIELD is a Londoner whose poems have appeared in *Salt and Honey* (with Martin Humphries, 1989) and in various anthologies.

PETER DANIELS grew up in Birmingham and is publisher of The Oscars Press, for which he edited *Take Any Train* (1990) and co-edited *Jugular Defences* (1994) with Steve Anthony; his own collections are *Peacock Luggage* (with Moniza Alvi, 1992) and *Be Prepared* (1994).

ROGER FINCH, who studied Music Theory at George Washington University and Near Eastern Languages at Harvard, teaches at Surguadai University, Saitama, Japan; his book of poems, *According to Lilies*, appeared in 1992.

ROBERT FRIEND, born in Brooklyn, settled in Israel in 1950 and taught English and American Literature at the Hebrew University in Jerusalem. He has published eight volumes of poetry, including *Somewhere Lower Down* (1980) and *The Next Room* (1995).

DINYAR GODREJ grew up in Indore, India, and was educated at St Xavier's College, Bombay, and St Anne's College, Oxford; his work appeared in *Twentysomething* (1992).

THOM GUNN was born in Kent and since 1954 has lived mostly in California. He has published nine collections of poems, as well as pamphlets and two collections of essays. His *Collected Poems* appeared in 1993.

JOHN HEATH-STUBBS is the author of numerous books of poetry – including *Collected Poems* (1988), *Sweetapple Earth* (1993) and *Galileo's Salad* (1996) – and an autobiography, *Hindsights* (1993).

ADAM JOHNSON was born in Stalybridge, Cheshire, and moved to London in 1984. His two collections of poetry, *The Spiral Staircase* (1993) and *The Playground Bell* (1994), appeared posthumously.

FRANCIS KING is a well-known, distinguished and prolific novelist who has also published a biography of E.M. Forster and edited the diaries of J.R. Ackerley; his less familiar poems were collected in a privately printed edition for distribution to his friends in 1996.

DAVID KINLOCH teaches at the University of Strathclyde; he is co-founder of the magazine *Verse* and author of *Dustie-fute* (1992) and *Paris-Forfar* (1995).

JAMES KIRKUP's first collection of poems, *The Drowned Sailor*, appeared in 1947, but his reputation was established by *The Prodigal Son* (1959). A prolific translator, he has lived since 1977 mostly in Japan and Andorra.

JOEL LANE was born in Exeter and grew up in Birmingham, where he still lives; his work has appeared in numerous magazines and anthologies.

J.D. MCCLATCHY, editor of *The Yale Review*, is the author of three collections of poems, a book of essays and several libretti.

EDWIN MORGAN taught at the University of Glasgow, retiring as titular Professor in 1980. His *Collected Poems* appeared in 1990 and his *Collected Translations* in 1996; his most recent book of poems is *Sweeping Out the Dark* (1994).

TIM NEAVE lives and works in Grimsby; his poems appeared in *Twentysomething* (1992).

WILFRED OWEN, the major English poet of the First World War, was killed in action on 4 November 1918.

SANDRO PENNA's poetry first appeared in a comprehensive English translation in *Remember Me, God of Love* (1993).

WILLIAM PLOMER was born in South Africa but eventually settled in Sussex; his novels include *Turbott Wolfe* (1925), set in Africa, *Sado* (1931), set in Japan, and the quintessentially English *Museum Pieces* (1952). His *Collected Poems* appeared in the final form in 1973.

NEIL POWELL is the author of four books of poetry, a novel, a study of contemporary English poetry and a critical biography, *Roy Fuller: Writer and Society* (1995). He lives in Suffolk.

LAWRENCE SCHIMEL is the editor of over a dozen anthologies, and his own work has appeared in numerous magazines and anthologies. He lives in Manhattan, where he writes and edits full time.

MICHAEL SCHMIDT, born in Mexico and educated at Harvard and Oxford, has lived for the past twenty-five years in Manchester, where he runs Carcanet Press and edits *PN Review* as well as lecturing at the University. His most recent book is *Selected Poems 1972–1997* (1997).

QUENTIN STEVENSON has recently returned to poetry after a long silence since his first collection in 1957; he lives in London.

STEPHEN TAPSCOTT is Professor of Literature at MIT. He has published several books of poetry in the USA as well as translating Neruda and editing *Twentieth-Century Latin American Poetry*. His first collection of poetry to appear in Britain is *From the Book of Changes* (1997).

IVOR C. TREBY is the author of *Woman with Camellias* (1995) and of poems in numerous magazines and anthologies.

R.M. VAUGHAN is the author of twelve plays and a collection of poems, *a selection of dazzling scarves* (1996). He lives partly in Toronto and partly in his native New Brunswick.

PAUL WILKINS published his first book of poems, *Pasts*, in 1979. He lives in Derry.

GREGORY WOODS, who teaches at Nottingham Trent University, is the author of *We Have the Melon* (1992); his *History of Gay Literature* is scheduled for publication in autumn 1997.

PETER WYLES has published poetry in various anthologies; he lives in Hertfordshire.

ACKNOWLEDGEMENTS

The editor and publishers are grateful for permission to include the following copyright material.

'After the Blitz, 1941' and 'Missing' by J.R. Ackerley: from *Micheldever & Other Poems* (Ian McKelvie, 1972), © 1972 The Estate of J.R. Ackerley, reprinted by permission of Francis King, Literary Executor.

'The Puerto Rican GoGo Boy' by Marc Almond: from *The Angel of Death in the Adonis Lounge* (GMP, 1988), © 1988 Marc Almond, reprinted by permission of GMP Publishers Ltd.

'Life Drawing' and 'A Good Fit' by Steve Anthony: © 1997 Steve Anthony, by permission of the author.

'Following a Man' by John Ash: from *Selected Poems* (Carcanet, 1996), © 1996 John Ash, reprinted by permission of Carcanet Press Ltd.

'XV', 'XLVIII' and 'XCIX' by Catullus, translated by C.H. Sisson: from *Collected Translations* (Carcanet, 1996), © 1996 C.H. Sisson, reprinted by permission of Carcanet Press Ltd.

'The Next Table' by C.P. Cavafy: from *Poems by C.P. Cavafy*, translated by John Mavrogordato (The Hogarth Press, 1951), © 1951 John Mavrogordato, reprinted by permission of Random House UK Ltd.

'A Private View' by Robert Cochrane: from *Accepted Forms of Beauty in the West* (The Bad Press, 1996), © 1996 Robert Cochrane, reprinted by permission of the author.

'Give Me Back My Man' and 'Gym Class of '67 (Summer of Love)' by Steve Cranfield: from *Salt and Honey* (GMP, 1989), reprinted by permission of GMP Publishers Ltd; 'The Testament' by Steve Cranfield: © 1997 Steve Cranfield, by permission of the author.

'Liverpool St' and 'Assessment' by Peter Daniels: © 1997 Peter Daniels, by permission of the author.

'Of Course I Do' by Iestyn Edwards: © 1997 Iestyn Edwards, by permission of the author.

'Effects' by Richard Essenden: © 1997 Richard Essenden, by permission of the author.

'The Rape of Ganymede' and 'A Publicity Photograph' by Roger Finch: from *According to Lilies* (Carcanet, 1992), © 1992 Roger Finch, reprinted by permission of Carcanet Press Ltd.

'Robert' by Forbes: from *The Gay Journal*, Number Two, © 1979.

'Shirts' by Robert Friend: from *The Next Room* (Menard, 1995), © 1995 Robert Friend, reprinted by permission of The Menard Press; from 'The Teacher and the Indian': © 1997 Robert Friend, by permission of the author.

'Anyone could succumb ...' by Dinyar Godrej: from *Twentysomething* (GMP, 1992), © 1992 by Dinyar Godrej, reprinted by permission of GMP Publishers Ltd.

'San Francisco Streets' by Thom Gunn: from *Collected Poems* (Faber, 1993), © 1982 Thom Gunn, by permission of Faber and

Faber Ltd and Farrar, Straus & Giroux Inc; 'The Problem' and 'In the Post Office': © 1992, 1997 Thom Gunn, by permission of the author.

'In Memory' by John Heath-Stubbs: from *Galileo's Salad* (Carcanet, 1996), © 1996 John Heath-Stubbs, reprinted by permission of Carcanet Press Ltd.

'Unscheduled Stop' by Adam Johnson: from *New Poetries* (Carcanet, 1994); 'Early November' and 'The Playground Bell': from *The Playground Bell* (Carcanet, 1994), © 1994 The Estate of Adam Johnson, reprinted by permission of Carcanet Press Ltd.

'Holiday', 'The Address' and 'The Bank-Notes' by Francis King: from *The Buried Spring* (privately printed, 1996): © 1996 Francis King, reprinted by permission of the author.

'In Brompton Cemetery' and 'Bed' by David Kinloch: © 1997 David Kinloch, by permission of the author.

'Homo in Omnibus' by James Kirkup: from *So Long Desired* (GMP, 1986), © 1986 James Kirkup, reprinted by permission of GMP Publishers Ltd.

'Michel Foucault' by Joel Lane: from *Jugular Defences* (Oscars Press, 1994), © 1994 Joel Lane, reprinted by permission of the author; 'The Outline of a House' and 'Sandman': © 1997 Joel Lane, by permission of the author.

'After Ovid' by J.D. McClatchy: from *After Ovid*, edited by Michael Hofmann and James Lasdun (Faber, 1994), © 1994 J.D. McClatchy, reprinted by permission of the author; 'Late Night Ode': © 1977 J.D. McClatchy, reprinted by permission of the author.

'Epigram XI.8' by Martial, translated by Anthony Reid, from

Roman Poets of the Early Empire (Penguin, 1991), © 1991, reprinted by permission of the translator.

'Christmas Eve' and 'Dear man, my love goes out in waves ... ' by Edwin Morgan: from *Collected Poems* (Carcanet, 1990), © 1990 Edwin Morgan, reprinted by permission of Carcanet Press Ltd; 'Tram-Ride, 1939 (F.M.)': from *Sweeping Out the Dark* (Carcanet, 1994), © 1994 Edwin Morgan, reprinted by permission of Carcanet Press Ltd.

'Poem: L.M.C.' by Tim Neave: from *Twentysomething* (GMP, 1992), © 1992 Tim Neave, reprinted by permission of GMP Publishers Ltd.

'I lose myself ... ' by Sandro Penna: from *Remember Me, God of Love*, translated by Blake Robinson (Carcanet, 1993), © 1993 Blake Robinson, reprinted by permission of Carcanet Press Ltd.

'Venetian Sonnets: XII' by August Graf von Platen-Hallermünde, translated by Edwin Morgan: from *Collected Translations* (Carcanet, 1996), © 1996 Edwin Morgan, reprinted by permission of Carcanet Press Ltd.

'A Casual Encounter' by William Plomer: from *Collected Poems* (Jonathan Cape, 1973), © 1973 William Plomer, reprinted by permission of Random House UK Ltd.

'The Difference' and 'Hundred River' by Neil Powell: from *The Stones on Thorpeness Beach* (Carcanet, 1994), © 1994 Neil Powell, reprinted by permission of Carcanet Press Ltd.

'Hampstead Notebook: The Boy with the Broken Arm' by Quentin Stevenson: © 1997 Quentin Stevenson, by permission of the author.

'Using the Poet's Bathroom' and 'Palimpsest' by Lawrence

Schimel: © 1997 Lawrence Schimel, by permission of the author.

'His father was a baker...' by Michael Schmidt: from *Selected Poems 1972–1997* (Smith/Doorstop Books, 1997), © 1997 Michael Schmidt, reprinted by permission of the author.

'The Queens' by Stephen Tapscott: from *From the Book of Changes* (Carcanet, 1997), © 1997 Stephen Tapscott, reprinted by permission of Carcanet Press Ltd.

'Incident on the Central Line' by Ivor C. Treby: © 1997 Ivor C. Treby, by permission of the author.

'10 Reasons Why I Fall in Love ...' by R.M. Vaughan: from *a selection of dazzling scarves* (ECW Press, 1996), © 1996 R.M. Vaughan, reprinted by permission of the author.

'My Tired Darlings' and 'Glasnost'' by Paul Wilkins: © 1997 Paul Wilkins, by permission of the author.

'A goatboy pissing ...' and 'Andy' by Gregory Woods: from *We Have the Melon* (Carcanet, 1992): © 1992 Gregory Woods, reprinted by permission of Carcanet Press Ltd; 'Reconciliation': © 1993 Gregory Woods, by permission of the author.

'Beauty' and 'Bird Flight' by Peter Wyles: © 1997 Peter Wyles, by permission of the author.

While every effort has been made to contact copyright-holders, the editor and publishers would be grateful to be notified of any errors or omissions in the above acknowledgements.

INDEX OF POETS

INDEX OF FIRST LINES